P9-CAJ-927

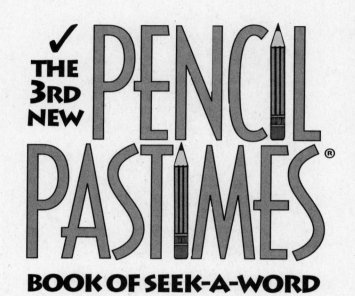

THE 3RD NEW PENCIL PASTIMES®

BOOK OF SEEK-A-WORD

THE 3RD NEW PENCIL PASTIMES®

BOOK OF SEEK-A-WORD

RICHARD MANCHESTER

BRISTOL PARK BOOKS

Copyright © 2005 by Crosstown Publications

All rights reserved. No part of this work may be
reproduced or transmitted in any form or by any means,
electronic or mechanical, including photocopying,
recording, or any information storage and retrieval
system, without permission in writing from the publisher.
All requests for permission in writing to reproduce
material from this Work should be directed to Crosstown
Publications, 475 Park Avenue South, New York,
NY 10016.

First Bristol Park Books edition published in 2005.

Bristol Park Books, Inc.
450 Raritan Center Parkway
Edison, NJ 08837

Bristol Park Books is a registered trademark of
Bristol Park Books, Inc.

Pencil Pastimes ® is a registered trademark of
Bristol Parks Books, Inc.

Published by arrangement with Crosstown Publications.

ISBN: 0-88486-375-1

Printed in the United States of America.

CONTENTS

PUZZLES

DRAMAS

The theater lights dim; the curtain goes up on our theatrical assortment—this "repertory" consists of classical and contemporary dramas and comedies, plus a few modern musicals. If you have never seen these works as plays, you might be familiar with those that have been adapted to film, opera, and television.

AJAX
ANATOL
ANTIGONE
APPLAUSE
ARI
BACCHAE
BECKET
BRAND
CABARET
CLAUDIA
CYCLOPS
DYLAN
ELECTRA
FAUST
GASLIGHT
GHOSTS
GIGI
GYPSY
HAIR
HAMLET
HARVEY
HELEN
HIGH TOR
HIPPOLYTUS
HOME
ION
JANE
KEAN
LUV
MACBETH
MAME
MEDEA
NOAH
ONDINE
RAIN
RHESUS
ROPE (The)
SLEUTH
STRIFE
TWIGS
WINTERSET
YERMA

```
E D H A R T C E L E M O H S
A N A E D E M R A N N O T R
H A O X Q S A I I A E E H O
C R N G P R L A D J L R T T
C B Y L I E R H U M E G E H
A H E L O T A N A A H K B G
B P V R S N N H L M C E C I
A N R U S I G A C E A A A H
R P A T G W X Y B N M N M E
E F H L A A C A P O R S O S
T N O I Y L S S J S E T R U
W X G I O D L L B A Y S H A
I I P P L E E N I D N O E L
G R S V U L P A M G E H S P
S S U T Y L O P P I H G U P
P O H A E Q R E F I R T S A
```

FLORIDA KEYS —————————————————— 2

Florida became United States territory in 1819, when it was ceded to us by Spain. For many years the keys—or chain of small islands off the southern tip of the mainland—were out of the way of tourists, but slowly many of them were built up into today's popular resorts. Below is a list of places to visit in the keys. We've circled BIG PINE to start you off.

ANCLOTE
BARNES
BIG PINE
BISCAYNE

BOOT
BUSH
CASEY
CHICKEN

CONCH
COQUINA
CRAB
CRAWFISH

CUTOE
DEER
DINNER
EAGLE
EGMONT
FIESTA
FISH HAWK
FRANK
HOWE
LAKE
LARGO
LONG
LONGBOAT
MUD
MULLET
OHIO
OYSTER
PACET
PERDIDO
RANKIN
ROSCOE
SANDS
SAWYER
SHELL
SIESTA
SNIPE
SPY
STAKE
VACA
WATER
WEST
WINDLEY
WOMAN

```
A Y E L D N I W S D N A S C
N T N C R A B O U Q C S R O
C O Y S T E R M B A E A E P
L H A H K F N A V N W K O A
O Y C E S Q R N R F A E C C
T D S N G U E A I L Y U S E
E C I P O N B S N D B O O T
H O B D I C H I C K E N R A
M Q T P R H A E Y K I E V O
V U G U A E P S A O T N R B
A I L W C I P T E A G L E G
B N K L N Y S A W Y E R N N
D A T S E I F C O I H O A O
E G M O N T L S H E L L W L
```

2

Although the movie industry has historically been based in Hollywood, Florida has had so many movies filmed there, this state has earned the nickname of Hollywood East. This puzzle contains stars who have made films in Florida.

1. ADAMS (Julie)
2. ALDA (Alan)
3. AMECHE (Don)
4. CRONYN (Hume)
5. CRUISE (Tom)
6. CULKIN (Macaulay)
7. DALTON (Timothy)
8. DANGERFIELD (Rodney)
9. DE NIRO (Robert)
10. DEPP (Johnny)
11. EASTWOOD (Clint)
12. FIELD (Sally)
13. GARR (Teri)
14. GLEASON (Jackie)
15. GRANT (Cary)
16. HESTON (Charlton)
17. HURT (William)
18. HUTTON (Betty)
19. IVES (Burl)
20. LAKE (Veronica)
21. LEWIS (Jerry)
22. PRESLEY (Elvis)
23. PRICE (Vincent)
24. QUAID (Dennis)
25. REED (Jerry)
26. REYNOLDS (Burt)
27. SEGAL (George)
28. SINATRA (Frank)
29. SNIPES (Wesley)
30. STEWART (James)
31. STIERS (David Ogden)
32. TORN (Rip)
33. WELCH (Raquel)
34. WIEST (Dianne)
35. WILLIAMS (Esther)
36. WOODARD (Alfre)
37. WOODS (James)
38. WYMAN (Jane)
39. WYNN (Keenan)

```
P C K A D O O W T S A E K A
G P D P R E S L E Y Q L M T
D L E A L E D V H L R E L C
A S E D G N I K L U C R T S
N M L A K E A N E H T H S D
G A L M S W U A E C L T R L
E I J S L O Q M R T I C O O
R L O C R O N Y N E R R L N
F L N R Z D L W R O R U P Y
I I T O I S S S J A T I H E
E W E L T N A R G W Q S L R
L Y R L I L E W I S I E E T
D N L P D R A D Z L J E O H
M N E R W O O D A R D R S L
C S S T E W A R T A N I S T
```

See film names at end of answer section.

Search for the 60 words hidden in the diagram below. Then, going left to right starting at the top of the diagram, read the uncircled letters to learn the name of a mechanic who invented the apple parer on St. Valentine's Day in 1803.

ALARM	BROOK	DINED	FEEBLE	HENCE
ANNEX	CANOE	DIRECT	FLAXEN	HUSKY
ARCTIC	CHAFF	DOUSE	FOLDED	KNEAD
BASIL	CHORE	DUPLEX	FRESH	LAMENT
BOWER	COCOA	EXERT	GENTLE	LIKEN
BREAD	CUCKOO	EXPAND	GLADE	LOFTY

MANATEE
MASON
MELEE
MUSSEL
NICER
OILED
OTTER
OWNER
POTPIE
PUDDING
PULSE
SERENE
SNARL
STAIN
STEAM
STEED
STEEP
STORY
SUMMER
SUNDAE
SWANK
TOKEN
TOPPLE
TUNIC
TURBAN
TUREEN
TWEET
UTTER
WOBBLE
YEAST

```
C H O R E M M U S S E L M G
I E E Y R O T S M L I K E N
N O S A M T W R O S P N L I
U N L U E A E N A S T E E D
T A U R N W E B E L O E E D
S C P K O D T T E R P X E U
N D E B N I A T S G P D S P
I E B R A N N E X A L F U L
C L K O I E A E N O E A O E
E I C O Y D M D F K L Y D X
R O T K T S C T U R B A N E
C O S C A T Y L A M E N T R
T U T U R E E N E R E S S T
H E N C E A S R B F F A H C
```

HIDDEN NUMBERS ———————————— 5

Did you know that the Chicago post office once rejected 25,000 coarse and vulgar St. Valentine's cards as being unfit to go through the mail?

5100	7413	8723
5121	7499	8744
5303	8511	8822
5344	8533	8843
5501	8633	8920
5542	8639	8941
5703		
5732		
5900		
5949		
6039		
6094		
6249		
6293		
6404		
6424		
6634		
6640		
6824		
6832		
7012		
7033		
7109		
7193		
7202		
7243		
7329		
7399		

```
1 8 5 1 1 6 3 4 1 8 9 0 3 6
1 2 4 9 1 2 2 0 4 2 6 2 6 2
4 0 1 3 0 3 1 4 7 3 1 3 4 9
4 2 3 5 7 8 9 6 9 3 4 4 3 3
7 5 3 5 6 4 7 0 9 4 9 5 0 9
8 5 1 0 0 9 0 2 4 5 2 1 9 1
1 2 0 6 3 0 8 6 3 9 0 4 7 9
5 2 4 4 9 4 3 0 3 0 7 5 3 0
3 2 7 5 1 6 3 4 6 2 0 4 3 1
4 2 3 9 5 6 2 0 1 8 5 5 0 1
4 3 2 9 0 8 9 7 0 9 3 2 7 6
1 0 9 8 3 4 9 9 0 4 2 2 3 8
2 3 9 4 8 3 4 2 7 1 0 1 4 2
7 1 0 9 8 8 4 3 0 2 2 9 0 4
```

SO YOU WANT TO BE IN PICTURES

Have you always wanted to be in the movies? Well, maybe you are already! If you're female, that is, because maybe your name is one of those left out below in movie titles that each contain a female name. Fill a name into each blank, then find that name in the diagram opposite. As a solving aid, the names to find are in alphabetical order. After you find them all, read the uncircled letters for a Shirley MacLaine quote about acting.

1. _____ of God
2. _____ Doesn't Live Here Anymore
3. _____ Hall
4. The Song of _____
5. Down and Out in _____ Hills
6. My Darling _____
7. Driving Miss _____
8. Hello, _____!
9. My Sister _____
10. The Americanization of _____
11. All About _____
12. _____ Girl
13. _____ Goes Hawaiian
14. _____ and Her Sisters
15. _____ La Douce
16. Whatever Happened to Baby _____?
17. The Prime of Miss _____ Brody
18. A Date With _____
19. Tell Me That You Love Me, _____ Moon

20. The Sons of _____ Elder
21. _____ Foyle
22. Eyes of _____ Mars
23. Presenting _____ Mars
24. Auntie _____
25. The Bells of St. _____'s
26. _____ Pierce
27. The Unsinkable _____ Brown
28. _____ Got Married
29. My Cousin _____
30. Educating _____
31. Broadway Danny _____
32. _____'s Baby
33. When Harry Met _____
34. Two Mules for Sister _____
35. _____, Queen of the Jungle
36. _____'s Choice
37. Breakfast at _____'s
38. Victor/_____

```
S I Y C A A L E H C A R R E A M
E A L O N R T A M R I E A S N B
N O R E J U N I E D U T O E N J
G L E A I N R F R E O P E A I U
A H V T A B E O O Y H L E C E D
S O E H T N D Y S I I J L D T Y
H E B C A E M L E E E E R Y N R
A L A U R A D L T H M E N A J A
Y A A D N G M A M E T A F H Y M
E L L L I I K S N F K F R G Y Y
E I L D V I C T O R I A R Y L S
M C G O T I I N F T E O T I I I
R E O T M N N T E V E B L I M A
T O Y F E U S Y G G E P I T E D
```

See names at end of answer section.

This is a Word Search in reverse. Circled letters are the initial letters of one or more words, and any letter may be part of more than one word. Fill in each word in a straight line without crossing any black squares; when you're done, every square will be filled. CHAFE has been entered for you.

ABEYANCE CHROMOSOME FASCINATED INSTEP

ABREAST CRUMPLE FEAST LACERATED

AVERSE DEEP GIGOLO LIBEL

BASIL DOCTOR GRAIN LOSS

BROIL EERIE HAPPIEST MANIFEST

~~CHAFE~~ ELEGANT HELD MOTH

CHAT ENTERED HEMOSTAT NOTABLE

OMNIPOTENT

PALEFACE

PICNIC

PORPOISE

RASCAL

REPREHENSIVE

ROCOCO

SEARCH

SERENADE

SPOILAGE

STIGMA

TEETH

TOPSOIL

TRAMP

VEND

WASH

WHETSTONE

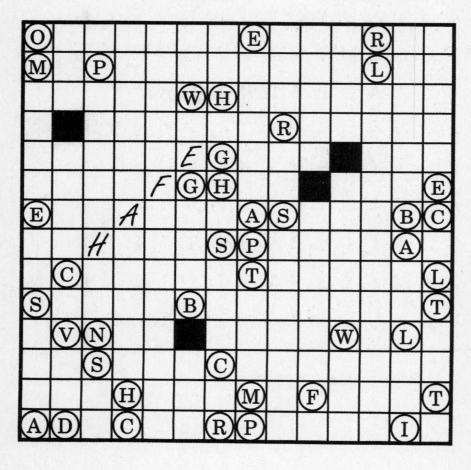

Scan the grid in all directions for 54 familiar words, arranged in pairs. Each word in a pair crosses its partner through the center letter, forming either a "+" or an "x" shape. There are 20 five-letter combinations and 7 seven-letter combinations to find. One pair has been circled to start you off.

YOUR WORD LIST

See word list at end of answer section.

In honor of Valentine's Day, we'd like to offer you a HEART—not once, but 44 times! See if you can find all the HEARTs in the diagram; and remember, we ♥ you!

```
T A H T T H E A T T R A E H
R R E R E T A R E R H R E T
A H A A H E A R T E A A H R
E E R E A E T R A T R E R A
H T T H H E A R T T R T H E
A E R E T E T E T R H A R H
T R A E H R R T R A E H E A
E R E R A H A R A T A A T H
T A H E T A E E E T R A E H
H E A R T E H A H T T A T E
A E H R A R E E R E R R E A
T R A E H E A R T T A A H R
H E A R T R R E H E A R E T
H E A R T A T R H E A R T H
```

WHEN IN ROME

Only the letters of the Roman numerals plus the five vowels have been used to make the words below.

CALVE
CAMEL
CAMEO
CEDED
CELLO
CIVIC
CIVIL
CLOUD
CLOVE
COCOA
CODED
COLIC
COMIC
COMMA
COULD
DEUCE
IVIED
LACED
LAMED
LEAVE
LEVEE
LEVEL
LIVED
LIVID
LLAMA
LOCAL
LOVED
MADAM

MAMMA
MAUVE
MAXIM
MEDAL
MELEE

MIMIC
MIXED
MODEL
MOVED
MOVIE

VALUE
VEXED
VILLA
VIOLA
VOICE

```
I C O D E D E V O M E L E E
C D E U C E M E L C V M V I
L O D I V I L D U O L C A L
L C U L O V M I I L A C E D
O L A L O I V C E I A E L E
C C D M D L E V M C V V M V
A I E L E M E C O E M A C O
L V M V X L V M L M E V I L
V I A I I L M M L D L C V M
A L L A M A E D E D E C I I
M I M A O L O D C D M X C E
M C D E V I L C O L A I E L
A A L L I V C D O M I L C V
M A U V E V O L C C I M O C
```

RECIPE: LOBSTER DE JONGHE

This is a delicious and attractive main dish to serve when you're having company. All of the terms in the list are taken directly from the recipe.

ABOUT
BEAT
BOIL
BOILING
BRANDY
BREAD
  CRUMBS
BROIL
BROWN
BUBBLY
BUTTER
CASSEROLES
CAYENNE
CHIVES
CONTROL
COOK

CREAM
CUP
CUT-UP
DASH
DIVIDE
EGG
FLOUR
GARLIC
GOLDEN
HALF
HEAT
HOT
INCHES
INDIVIDUAL
INGREDIENTS
LIGHT

LOBSTER
MARGARINE
MEDIUM
MELT
MELTED
MINCED
MINUTES
MIXTURE
ONION
OVEN
PAPRIKA
PARSLEY
PEPPER
RED PEPPER
REMOVE
RICE

SALT
SAUCE
SAUCEPAN
SNIPPED
SOFT
SPRINKLE
STIR
TABLESPOON
TEASPOON
TOPPING
TOSS
UNTIL
WORCESTER-
  SHIRE
YOLKS

Lobster de Jonghe

3 tablespoons butter or
  margarine
3 tablespoons flour
2¼ cups light cream
¼ cup + 2 tablespoons brandy
1 teaspoon salt
Dash cayenne red pepper
2 egg yolks
4 cups cut-up cooked lobster

3 to 4 cups hot cooked rice
½ cup melted butter or margarine
1 cup soft bread crumbs
1 clove garlic, minced
1 tablespoon minced green onion
  or chives
1½ teaspoons paprika
½ teaspoon Worcestershire sauce
Parsley with stems snipped off

Melt 3 tablespoons butter in saucepan. Stir in flour. Cook over low heat, stirring until bubbly, about two minutes. Remove from heat. Stir in 2 cups of the cream, the brandy, salt and pepper. Heat to boiling, stirring constantly. Boil and stir 1 minute. Remove from heat.

Beat egg yolks with ¼ cup cream. Slowly stir at least half the hot mixture into the egg mixture; blend egg mixture into remaining hot mixture in saucepan. Cook sauce over medium heat, stirring constantly, 2 minutes. Stir in lobster; heat through. Divide hot rice among 8 individual casseroles; top with lobster mixture. Toss ½ cup butter and the remaining ingredients; sprinkle on casseroles. Set oven control at broil. Broil casseroles about 5 inches from heat 4 to 5 minutes or until topping is golden brown. Garnish with parsley.

```
S B M U R C D A E R B U B B L Y R
T L G U N T E A S P O O N G G E I
N I N S I D E L K N I R P S P C C
E O I E I D E P P I N S E P O A E
I R L V L P E P P E R C E N V R N
D B I I O S A M E U U P T T E T I
E D O H B N E R O A D R A M N U R
R A B C S L I L S E O B O P W O A
G S I S T R F O R L L V T A E B G
N H N E E N E W N E E R I T S A R
I Y D H R E A T S C M Y I A R S A
P D I C A D T P S R I O L L P E M
P N V N Y L O C T E N T I I U T I
O A I I E O F O F A C C O G T U X
T R D M N G L O O M E R B H U N T
O B U T T E R K S P D H O T C I U
S N A P E C U A S U B R O W N M R
S E L O R E S S A C A Y E N N E E
```

TAIL TAG

Solve this puzzle by forming a chain of circled words in which the last letter of one word is the first letter of the next. The number in parentheses tells you the length of the word you're looking for. We have provided PRIME to start you off.

PRIME _____ (5)   _____ (5)   _____ (5)
E _____ (6)   _____ (5)   _____ (4)
_____ (4)   _____ (6)   _____ (4)
_____ (7)   _____ (4)   _____ (5)
_____ (6)   _____ (4)   _____ (4)
                                        _____ (4)
                                        _____ (4)
                                        _____ (5)
                                        _____ (4)
                                        _____ (6)
                                        _____ (4)
                                        _____ (4)
                                        _____ (5)
                                        _____ (5)
                                        _____ (4)
                                        _____ (6)
                                        _____ (5)
                                        _____ (5)
                                        _____ (6)
                                        _____ (4)
                                        _____ (5)
                                        _____ (7)
                                        _____ (6)
                                        _____ (4)
                                        _____ (4)
                                        _____ (4)
                                        _____ (4)
                                        _____ (5)
                                        _____ (4)

```
O A G Y R H T D O R M E R P
C L R Z E A E N E M A O P R
T U O O B P C T I Z L Z Q I
E H Z S M G F K R L Q R E M
T Y C A U A Z I M E E T S E
H I T T L R D L B O D M C S
G S M A E L T T A B L H O Q
N S G E H Z R R U Q R D R R
M E Q E C U H T T S U R T T
L R L Z N R S O Z S H Y Y Z
L P G K E E N E T V L O O W
I H L N L I M I I R I L H O
T T H G C F N G C R F V H R
S E B O L G L B Z E T H I C
```

See word list at end of answer section.

14

JACKPOT ———————————— 13

To solve this puzzle, insert a letter from below into each of the circles in the diagram. This letter should be one that will let you form as many 5-letter words as possible. If you have entered the correct letters into the circles, you should be able to find 51 words in total. We've inserted the letter "T" to start you off.

| C | F | H | K | L | N | P | R | S | T | V |

YOUR WORD LIST

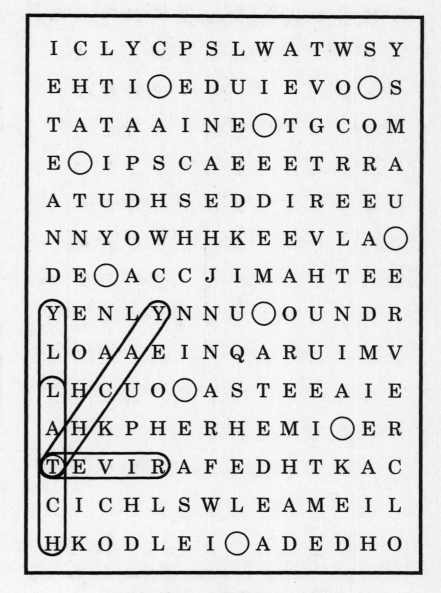

See word list at end of answer section.

Armored cavalry emerged as the premier fighting force during the Battle of Hastings (1066) when armored Norman horsemen defeated the numerically superior but unarmored English foot soldiers. Armored protection had long been in use; the armored warrior's closet would include the following items.

```
V K N P A L L E T T E T E L
A R T O B U A E B M A J A O
M E G A R I L T A C E M T N
B B D N S T E M R A B U O I
R U B R N S S E N O I R O M
A A T U A E E A Y L D T S T
C H A U S S E S L L C A M E
E G O S D O S E U P U S C N
C R I U P L Y A H B I A A O
B U T N I L P S R E R L S G
C E L G R E A V E B A L Q R
S U A E K R S S E B S E U U
O H C V T E L R A L S T E B
G O R G E T E T E N I S A B
V N O E G R E B A H S D E N
```

ARMET
BASINET
BEAVER
BRASSARD
BURGONET
CASQUE
CHAUSSES
CUIRASS
CUISSE
CULET
GAUNTLET
GORGET
GREAVE
HABERGEON
HAUBERK
JAMBEAU
LAMBOY
MORION
NASAL
PALLETTE
PAULDRON
PLASTRON
REREBRACE
SALLET
SOLLERET
SPLINT
TACE
TASSES
TUILLE
VAMBRACE

If you stretch the truth a bit, would that be a baldachin or a taradiddle? Some words, no matter how much fun to say, have fallen out of use. Here are a few of these seldom-used gems. By the way, a baldachin is an ornamental canopy—and that's no taradiddle!

AOUL (gazelle)
AWETO (black pigment)
BABALA (pearl millet)
BABU (Hindu gentleman)
FOO DOG (decorative lion)
FYKE (fishnet bag)
GIGAS (flowering plant)
GYLE (brew)
KOKAKO (crow)
LICUALA (palm)
OUBLIETTE (dungeon)
POZZOLANA (volcanic ash)
SCRAY (tern)
SKEP (farm basket)
SNIGGLE (fish for eels)
THURIFER (incense holder)
TOKAY (house lizard)
TUCKAHOE (rootstock)
UCKERS (form of pachisi)
ULOTRICHAN (crisp hair)
UMIAK (Eskimo boat)
UNCO (stranger)
URHEEN (Chinese fiddle)
WAPATOO (edible tuber)
WAYZGOOSE (printers' holiday)

WHID (move silently)
WITLOOF (chicory)
WITWALL (woodpecker)
WOBBEGONG (carpet shark)

WOUGH (rock wall)
WOWSER (puritanical person)
YAKKA (work)
ZAREBA (stockade)

```
O L O A N A L O Z Z O P O E
O E K Y F R D I H W R W A U
T U R H E E N H C E A T M N
A T O S C R A Y F U L I H C
P K W C T I W I T W A L L G
A O N O N T R U C K B L B N
W K K Z Z U A B E R A Z A O
L A F C H C G S K E B H B G
Y K Y T T K Y A N N C T U E
A O F Z O A L W G I G A S B
K W O U G H E E R A G K O B
K H O F O O L T I W E G A O
A I D Y N E O O Z P O Z L W
L U O A N L A S R E K C U E
O N G O U B L I E T T E T Y
```

STREETS OF CHEYENNE ———————————————— 16

Cheyenne, Wyoming, sprang up when the Union Pacific Railroad selected it as the site for a division point in 1867. The exploration of the Black Hills gold fields in the 1870's stimulated the city's growth. Cheyenne is situated in the southeastern corner of Wyoming and is the state's capital. The list below consists of 39 streets of Cheyenne.

ACACIA   BUFFALO   CARLIN   COLLEGE
ANTELOPE CABLE   CENTRAL   CUSTER
ARAPAHO   CAPITOL   CINDY   DEER
BIG HORN CAREY   CLARK   DILLON
                               DONA
                               FOYER
                               FRONTIER
                               GLENDO
                               HAPPY JACK
                               HILLTOP
                               HOUSE
                               IDAHO
                               LARAMIE
                               MAIN
                               MOORE
                               O'NEIL
                               OSAGE
                               PAWNEE
                               PRAIRIE
                               REED
                               RIDGE
                               RUSSELL
                               SHOSHONI
                               THOMES
                               UTAH
                               WARREN
                               ZUNI

```
L T C R E T S U C E L B A C
I M A R E E D I H A U H O L
E O R E I T N O R F R L Q A
N O L L I D U P F O L E K R
O R I L Y S G A O E S R Y A
C E N L E H L E G T A A R M
A N T E L O P E S L L E G I
N R L S K S H E C M E L B E
R E A S D H M A A D P N I P
O Y R U L O T I P A C R D H
H O T R H N N V H A I R A O
G F N T A I C A C A R N H F
I X E E N W A P R J T A O M
B K C A J Y P P A H Z U N I
```

18

The New Orleans Mardi Gras pageants were held as early as 1827. It was not until 1857, however, that the distinctive carnival revelry now associated with the Mardi Gras was introduced.

The words "Mardi Gras" are French and mean "Fat Tuesday." They allude to an old ceremony in which a fat ox, symbolizing the passing of meat, was paraded through French cities on Shrove Tuesday, the day before the beginning of Lent and its forty days of fasting.

```
O G N I Z I L O B M Y S M C
X F N W G N I T S A F C I Z
T O A I A E Y A D E H T D B
E S T W S W M S Y T I O E E
V Y Y A D S E U T E T F D G
O A A N F U A H S M O M A I
R D A R T A T P C R A E R N
H E F R E N C H E I N A A N
S D R O W E H T R H H T P I
N U E D L M H O E O T W Y N
O L N G N E E H M L U E N G
G L C R T A F A O D H G D I
R A H A O F L E N T L E H U
A I T S F O R T Y I D R A M
```

PHRASE PLAY

Welcome to PHRASE PLAY. Each column below represents a portion of an old cliché or a familiar phrase. Column A is the beginning, Column B is the middle, and Column C is the end. See if you can pick an entry from each column to complete a common phrase. After you have connected all the phrases, you can then find each column entry in the diagram.

A	B	C
AS MUCH FUN	AS A BARREL	ABOUT
AS THE	CROW	BANG
BETTER	FELLOW	BOOK
COLD HANDS	FOR THE	CIRCLE
COME	FULL	END
FINISH	HIGH ON	EVILS
GET ALL	LIKE A	FLIES
GO OFF	MONEY WHERE	HEART
HAIL	OF TWO	MARINES
IN APPLE	PIE	MOON
KEEP IT	ROOM TO	OF MONKEYS
LIVE	SAFE	ORDER
NOT ENOUGH	STEAMED UP	SWING A CAT
OFF THE	THE DEEP	THAN SORRY
PUT YOUR	TOP OF	THE HOG
READ SOMEONE	TO THE	WELL MET
SHOOT	UNDER	YOUR HAT
TELL IT	WARM	YOUR HEAD
THE LESSER	WITH A	YOUR MOUTH IS

```
G E R E H W Y E N O M B A N G T T
O L H A Y R R O S N A H T C R A M
B W I S E O T H U W I T H A H A C
A L T D I M U F O R T H E R R O D
S T R F O N H O S A M H U I M G E
A O E O O C I F H G U O N E T O N
B S R M U E L F O G Y E U B N O O
A T A M L I P T O E S E C T O F E
R E S S E L E H T T E V I L H F M
R A E S A L E E K A E W R P G I O
E M O O N F D W M L O L C H I T S
L E T G O H E H T L R L L D H D D
M D N I B L H O W E E U E I N A A
I U F O P O T W T V D F O A T E E
A P O P B E E T O I N W H Y E H R
E K A S T H E H Y L U D A C T R G
K N T U O B A K T S L D B R L U Y
I S Y E K N O M F O W E A O M O P
L K S W I N G A C A T O F W S Y E
```

See phrases at end of answer section.

GARDENING WORDS ───────────────────────

''Mary, Mary, quite contrary, how does your garden grow?'' If you're not already a devotee of digging and planting, this puzzle might put you in a nature-nurturing mood.

ANISE	HYDRANGEA	RAKE
ANNUALS	INSECTICIDE	RHODODENDRON
APHIDS	IRIS	ROCKS
BEES	IVY	ROOTS
BERGAMOT	LEAF	ROSES
BLOSSOMS	LILY	SAP
BUD	LOAM	SEEDS
BULB	LOBELIA	SOD
DAHLIA	MOSS	SOIL
FENCE	MOWER	SPADE
FLAGSTONES	PAIL	SPRINKLER
FUCHSIA	PANSIES	TREES
GLOVES	PEONY	TROWEL
HEDGE	POD	URN
HERBS	POOL	VINE
HOE	POPPY	WEEDS
HOSE	POTS	ZINNIA

```
H O P B L O S S O M S H S S Y I
R E U E O C F N W Q L E W O R T
H Y D R A N G E A Z E R V I N E
O D K G M J E K N R S B S L F E
D M N A E D E E T C E S X U L D
O A M M S H O S E Y E A C I A I
D S T O O R L K P O D H V H G C
E T W T W A E O H A S Y L E S I
N W S A U E T R B I D I S E T T
D E M N R S R U A E A E I G O C
R P N O N O L N S G L S B E N E
O A C Y S B I D L Y N I B E E S
N K K E L S I O P A Y L A D S N
S M S E E H V P P M L O O P U I
N X A R P E O N Y Z I N N I A B
Y F X A S P R I N K L E R D O S
```

You may have noticed that we often write something here that uses several words in the word list. Here goes: The MINSTREL in the MAUVE SUEDE LEOTARD sang FALSETTO without RETICENCE as he MOVEd his DERRIERE onto the ALABASTER COVERLET. And you thought ours was a WEARISOME task!

AGREED	COVERLET	FULLY	MAUVE
ALABASTER	DART	GUARDIAN	MINSTREL
ASPEN	DERRIERE	IGNITED	MOVE
BATTALION	ERRAND	INDELIBLE	NASCENT
BLANKLY	EXEMPTION	LEOTARD	OCCUR
CAPON	FALSETTO	LIABLE	OPTIMAL
CLEFT	FLAMBE	LIMPID	PECAN
			PIECE
			PLEDGE
			PROPELLER
			REALTOR
			RETICENCE
			SERRATED
			SOFTIE
			SPECIMEN
			SUEDE
			TRANQUIL
			TRELLIS
			TROUNCE
			VESSEL
			WEARISOME

ODD-NUMBER SYMBOL SEARCH ———————— 21

This puzzle is constructed with numbers and symbols instead of words. The 25 combinations listed below consist of one number plus four symbols.

1 & : * –
+ 1 % ? /
= $ 1 # @
& / = 1 ?
$: @ – 1
3 + # % *
? 3 $ = :
% 3 & +
– @ / 3 $
* ? – @ 3
5 # & / =
% 5 * + &
: – 5 $ %
@ * ? 5 #
/ = + : 5
7 $ * – ?
7 & @ /
: % 7 = *
+ @ / 7 $
& # – : 7
9 ? % + @
* 9 = & –
/ : 9 # %
= & $ 9 +
? * @ / 9

```
+ 9 9 + ? + 7 : = $ 3 ? % @
$ # ? 1 = / & / 5 * 3 $ * 9
7 / 7 % 1 & & 3 = 3 ? ? = ?
& : – ? + # * 7 % 1 5 – – #
@ 9 = / 5 @ % $ 5 # 1 * @ 7
& # – : 7 : # ? 5 1 $ 9 – 3
% % 1 % 5 * + & : 7 / = = +
/ 3 & $ – # 3 5 + 9 ? & 7 1
@ & : 9 = @ 3 @ = 1 $ – 5 –
& ? * @ / 9 / 9 / 9 @ : 5 @
7 1 – : * 7 @ 3 + % $ 5 – :
# 7 $ 3 $ / ? 5 $ : * 3 + $
```

The longest sentence ever published appears in Victor Hugo's *Les Miserables.* It is 823 words long, and takes up three pages.

16344	18030	20443
16450	18465	20969
17345	19404	21365
17506	19596	21904
		22403
		22569
		23034
		23436
		73069
		73369
		75033
		75345
		77054
		77343
		79065
		79390
		80466
		80564
		82030
		82033
		84035
		84401
		88344
		88569

```
8 4 4 0 1 4 3 3 9 2 0 9 6 9
5 6 4 9 0 9 6 0 3 7 4 9 6 4
3 5 4 4 9 6 3 5 0 0 6 5 3 4
0 0 6 5 4 3 0 3 2 5 2 0 5 4
4 8 3 0 6 3 6 3 0 2 0 8 5 3
8 4 8 0 4 5 6 4 3 5 9 0 6 8
5 6 1 3 0 9 0 1 3 3 7 7 6 8
3 9 7 5 6 5 6 0 9 7 3 9 4 9
0 7 3 5 0 9 4 4 4 8 5 3 5 0
2 3 4 1 3 2 8 6 1 9 2 9 6 5
0 3 5 8 2 4 8 7 1 3 4 0 6 5
4 6 4 0 3 5 5 2 1 9 0 4 3 9
4 9 9 3 4 0 6 5 9 0 8 6 0 0
3 6 0 0 6 3 9 6 2 1 3 6 5 3
```

This puzzle contains 17 eight-letter terms, each with a number following it in parentheses, which refers to the numbered dashes below. Each word will form a box, reading either clockwise or counterclockwise. (BRIGHTEN has already been boxed to start you off.) As you find each term in the diagram, enter the letter in the middle of each box on the corresponding dash below the diagram ("O" has already been entered.) When you have finished, the letters on the dashes will spell out another name for the Mount Rushmore National Memorial.

BRIGHTEN (7)

CLOWNISH (15)

DARKROOM (17)

DISCOVER (2)

ELEPHANT (8)

EXCHANGE (4)

FASTENER (13)

HALLMARK (16)

MADRIGAL (10)

OBSOLETE (5)

ORDINARY (12)

PAVILION (11)

POSTCARD (3)

STERLING (6)

STROLLER (1)

VESTMENT (14)

VOCALIST (9)

```
I R B E N E R L H A G I
C X E R C T E I S L E R
H I E F A S G N L M A D
A N G H T E H O L C R O
L L I O E T I W A H K B
I S R B N E T N I S T E
V E R S O L F A V G I R
O L S T C E P H T M E L
C L O R A D M I S R N H
O N P D R Y O R E V T S
I M A R K R O D H O D I
L I V P H A N I S C A L
```

___ ___ ___ ___ ___ ___   O___ ___   ___ ___ ___ ___ ___ ___ ___ ___ ___
 1   2   3   4   5   6   7   8   9 10 11 12 13 14 15 16 17

Using the "M" in the word PROM, the first word in our list, try to find the second puzzle word which begins where the first word ends. Each word thereafter will be formed in the same way. Sharpen your skills because there are more Tail Tags coming up!

PROM _____ (4)   _____ (4)   _____ (4)
_____ (5)   _____ (4)   _____ (5)
_____ (5)   _____ (4)   _____ (5)
_____ (8)   _____ (5)   _____ (5)
                                                 _____ (4)
                                                 _____ (4)
                                                 _____ (7)
                                                 _____ (5)
                                                 _____ (4)
                                                 _____ (4)
                                                 _____ (4)
                                                 _____ (5)
                                                 _____ (4)
                                                 _____ (5)
                                                 _____ (4)
                                                 _____ (4)
                                                 _____ (4)
                                                 _____ (4)
                                                 _____ (6)
                                                 _____ (4)
                                                 _____ (5)
                                                 _____ (4)
                                                 _____ (4)
                                                 _____ (5)
                                                 _____ (4)
                                                 _____ (5)
                                                 _____ (4)
                                                 _____ (5)
                                                 _____ (5)
                                                 _____ (4)
                                                 _____ (4)

```
B X J K L Y K L I M P L E K
C M Y W A O W W A H R I N C
M Y O R Z P W E K L N J L O
G H D L I T T E R M O R P L
G G B A H S B I R U Z Z E D
Y U R E T S Z S G S M V W I
G O S H W E D L E I Y P L R
A D A O L A X U L C L I N G
H Q R Q H E R Z E A Z J Y R
S T O C C R E D N S L U S H
H Y Z I O Y R K T Y H T R A
Z E L M O A Z R A S B Y X V
M E L I L H Z K Z A X Q R E
R E M M I L S Y Q E G D U N
```

See word list at end of answer section.

The words in the Bingo card make up your word list. Find as many words as you can in the diagram, crossing them off the Bingo card as you go. When you have found all the words you can find, use the uncircled letters to form the single five-letter word, which, when crossed off the Bingo card, will give you BINGO, which is five words in a row, across, down or diagonally. Hint: There will be 2 letters remaining after you find the Bingo word. PERIL has been circled to start you off.

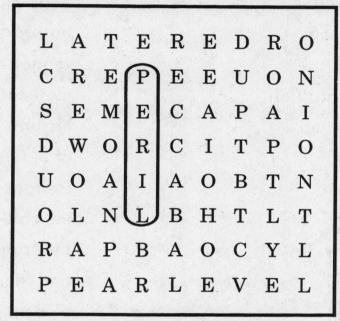

```
L  A  T  E  R  E  D  R  O
C  R  E  P  E  E  U  O  N
S  E  M  E  C  A  P  A  I
D  W  O  R  C  I  T  P  O
U  O  A  I  A  O  B  T  N
O  L  N  L  B  H  T  L  T
R  A  P  B  A  O  C  Y  L
P  E  A  R  L  E  V  E  L
```

Bingo Word: _____ _____ _____ _____ _____

B	I	N	G	O
ABACK	CABAL	PANIC	ONION	LATER
ABBOT	CHARM	PEARL	OPERA	LEVEL
APACE	CLASP	~~PERIL~~	OPTIC	LOTTO
APTLY	CREPE	PROUD	ORBIT	LOTUS
ARCED	CROWD	PUNCH	ORDER	LOWER

TEA TIME

Iced tea was introduced in 1904 at the International Exposition in St. Louis. Here is an account of how that refreshing beverage became popular.

Richard
Blechynden,
a Britisher,
visited
the Exposition
and set up
a stall
where
he sold
"dainty
cups
of the
very best
English tea."
However,
the weather
was so hot
that
customers
were few.
Faced
with the
bleak
prospect
of going
broke, the
vendor dumped
ice into
his urn
of hot tea.
He tasted
the cold
beverage
and found it
pleasing.
Soon
crowds
were
flocking
to his
stand
and a
new
food
fashion
was born.

```
S W G N I O G F O C H D Y E M V P
D R A H C I R C O R L E N H T O L
E N A S C U P S D O J W R T H K E
H D A N S M T R C W D E O E E U A
T J B T D O Y E O D H R B K W A S
H S L E S S H M R S L E S O E E I
T F E M O T E O I E P F A R A T N
I A A B F F T T I H E W B T H G
W C K O Y H I S U R N W C Y H S K
V E N D O R D U M P E D L T E I H
A D S T B L E C H Y N D E N R L E
S W T A H D T V F L O C K I N G T
T E L U L W I C E I N T O A D N A
A P N O I H S A F W I S M D C E S
L J S X N O I T I S O P X E E H T
L E G A R E V E B O T H A T I N E
H S I H O T I D N U O F D N A O D
```

MATH FUN

Here's a puzzle of a different sort. To solve, first complete each of the simple arithmetic problems in order, from left to right. Then write the answer in the space provided and search for that word in the diagram. We've done number 7 to show you what we mean. Warning: If you're looking for six, be careful not to circle part of sixty or sixteen. Answers may be repeated.

1. $47 + 36 - 21 =$ _____

2. $125 \div 5 \div 5 =$ _____

3. $6 \times 22 \div 12 =$ _____

4. $19 + 34 - 45 =$ _____

5. $49 \times 3 \div 21 =$ _____

6. $16 - 9 + 29 =$ _____

7. $9 \times 15 \div 45 =$ THREE

8. $23 + 99 - 39 =$ _____

9. $15 \times 15 \div 45 =$ _____

10. $36 \times 5 \div 3 =$ _____

11. $104 - 89 + 16 =$ _____

12. $12 \times 19 - 155 =$ _____

13. $15 \times 25 \div 75 =$ _____

14. $73 + 24 - 36 =$ _____

15. $18 \times 9 \div 81 =$ _____

16. $36 \div 18 \times 2 =$ _____

17. $82 - 64 + 19 =$ _____

18. $17 + 29 + 43 =$ _____

19. $72 \times 12 \div 144 =$ _____

20. $14 + 28 - 39 =$ _____

21. $102 - 87 + 65 =$ _____

22. $32 \times 5 \div 4 =$ _____

23. $48 - 19 - 24 =$ _____

24. $280 \div 140 \times 35 =$ _____

25. $62 - 54 + 9 =$ _____

26. $13 + 21 - 29 =$ _____

27. $17 + 46 + 19 =$ _____

28. $42 - 25 - 14 =$ _____

29. $11 \times 42 \div 22 =$ _____

```
T R S U S A X S E L E V E N
L E R E E E I O E V E V T O
Y T N E V E S Y T R I H T W
T N R I E E Z I E F G F O O
H H F Y N F N N X I H W O S
T W E N T Y O N E T T O I I
F N N Y Y Y T R O Y Y X W X
X I S Y T R I H T T T T T T
N F V R H H U H G Y H H W Y
Y I I E R T G O Z I R R R O
R H N V E I A I F E E I E N
T W E N E E T N E V E S S E
```

See number list at end of answer section.

TITLES OF RANK

The list below consists of 30 terms which denote a rank. Can you find each title, from BARON to VISCOUNT, in the diagram on the opposite page?

BARON	EMPEROR
BARONESS	KHAN
BARONET	KING
CAVALIER	KNIGHT
COUNT	LADY
COUNTESS	LORD
CZAR	MAHARANI
CZAREVNA	MARCHIONESS
CZARINA	MARQUIS
DAME	PRINCE
DON	PRINCESS
DUCHESS	QUEEN
DUKE	SHEIK
EARL	SQUIRE
EMIR	VISCOUNT

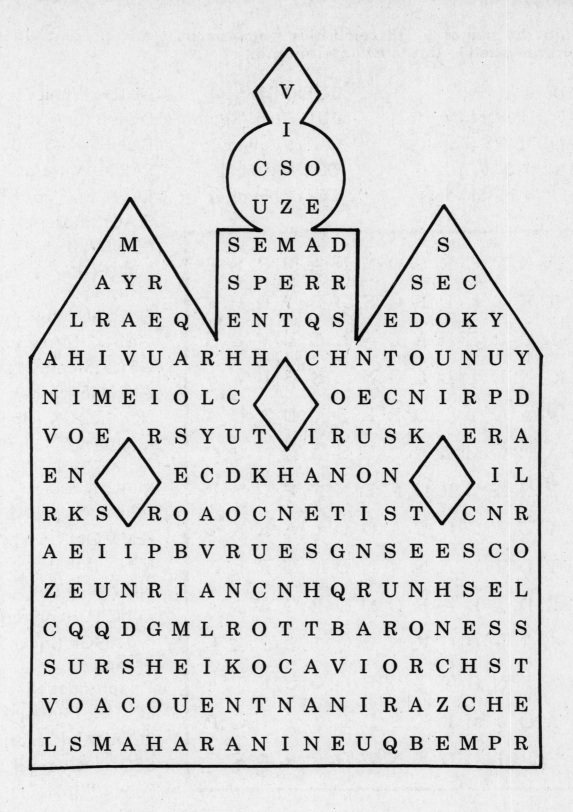

```
                    V
                    I
              C    S    O
              U    Z    E
        M        S E M A D        S
        A Y R    S P E R R    S E C
      L R A E Q  E N T Q S  E D O K Y
    A H I V U A R H H   C H N T O U N U Y
    N I M E I O L C     O E C N I R P D
    V O E   R S Y U T   I R U S K   E R A
    E N     E C D K H A N O N       I L
    R K S   R O A O C N E T I S T   C N R
    A E I I P B V R U E S G N S E E S C O
    Z E U N R I A N C N H Q R U N H S E L
    C Q Q D G M L R O T T B A R O N E S S
    S U R S H E I K O C A V I O R C H S T
    V O A C O U E N T N A N I R A Z C H E
    L S M A H A R A N I N E U Q B E M P R
```

BIRTHDAYS IN FEBRUARY

Find the names of 38 celebrities from the past and present whose birthdays fall in this late winter month.

ADLER (Larry)
ANDERSON (Marian)
ANDREWS (Patti)
BACKUS (Jim)
BERMAN (Shelley)

BONO (Sonny)
BUTTONS (Red)
CASH (Johnny)
CLARK (Dane)
COLE (Natalie)

CULLEN (Bill)
DOMINO (Fats)
DUNCAN (Sandy)
FARROW (Mia)
FAWCETT (Farrah)
FLACK (Roberta)
FONDA (Peter)
FORD (Tennessee Ernie)
FRIEDAN (Betty)
GABOR (Zsa Zsa)
GETZ (Stan)
GREENE (Lorne)
HOLBROOK (Hal)
KENNEDY (George)
KING (Carole)
KORMAN (Harvey)
LEMMON (Jack)
MILLS (John)
NOVAK (Kim)
O'NEILL (Jennifer)
PALANCE (Jack)
PETERS (Bernadette)
POITIER (Sidney)
ROMERO (Cesar)
SEGAL (George)
TORN (Rip)
TRAVOLTA (John)
WAGNER (Robert)

```
A N D E R S O N N A M R E B
T K C A L F O S R E T E P R
L G R E H A L N E O L V E H
O N E I L L G N I K B L W S
V A N T I O E E S M D A U A
A C G M Z E C U S A O N G C
R N A M R O K E N N E D Y E
T U W G O C A O C L A R K C
T D J L A N V N O M M E L N
E D X B A R O M E R O W G A
C F R D U K N B P T B S X L
W S N O T T U B O Q U L T A
A O J M F K S R E I T I O P
F R I E D A N W O R R A F H
```

On the Inauguration Day of January 20, 1961, these famous words were spoken: "My fellow Americans, ask not what your country can do for you; ask what you can do for your country. My fellow citizens of the world, ask not what America will do for you, but what together we can do for the freedom of man." After you have solved the puzzle, the uncircled letters will spell out the speaker.

ADJUST
ALIEN
ARSON
BEYOND
BUYER
CIRCULAR
CLEAR
CLUNG
COMEDY
CREST
CUTLET
DAUGHTER
DEUCE
DEVISE
DINER
EJECT
ETHER
EXPLODE
FLOSS
GARNISH
GLORY
GUESS
HONEY
INTACT
JAMBOREE
LEARN
LUCID
MAJESTY
MONEY
MUSIC
NATTY
PRETEXT
RAGWEED
RICKETY

RUSTLE
SIREN
SNIDE
SOUGHT
SPADE

SPRUNG
STOCK
SURGE
TASTE
TAUNT

TIPTOP
TRITE
TUGBOAT
TURRET
TUXEDO

TWINE
UNCLE
UPPER
USURY
UTMOST

```
B T H G U O S B U Y E R G M
E X P L O D E X U T A J U O
Y E N O M R N E H E M S E H
O T O R T E E E L K I O S T
N E S Y C P R C T C H I S Y
D R R E E P I N D I N E R T
E P A D J U S T E R R U T R
V G A E E A W U A C S T F E
I P R C L I M G N U L C S T
S P R U N G W B K L N A S H
E N C E S E E O O A N T O G
N I I D E T S A T R O N L U
D L E D T E L T U C E I F A
A C O M E D Y E K Y D E Y D
```

One of literature's most memorable characters is SCARLETT O'HARA from Margaret Mitchell's *Gone With the Wind*. Clever, self-centered, and determined, Scarlett uses sheer strength of will to salvage her life and her loved ones from the ashes of the Civil War. Scarlett's life was too powerful to die; today her story lives on in *Scarlett*, the sequel written by Alexandra Ripley. Here are many of the women found in this book.

ALICE (Harrington)
ALICIA (Savage)
ANNE (Hampton)
ANNIE (Doyle)
BEATRICE (Tarleton)

CAMILLA (Tarleton)
CARREEN
CAT
CELIE
CLARE (O'Hara)

COOKIE
DILCEY
ELEANOR (Butler)
ELLA
EMMA (Anson)
EMMA (Fulwich)
EULALIE (Aunt)
HETTY (Tarleton)
INDIA (Wilkes)
JANE (Benteen)
JULIA (Ashley)
KATHLEEN
LUTIE
MAMIE (Bart)
MAMMY
MARIE (Mrs.)
MARY (Telfair)
MAY (Taplow)
MINNIE (Wentworth)
MRS. FITZ
NAN (Sutcliffe)
OLD KATIE SCARLETT
PANSY
PAULINE (Aunt)
PEGEEN (O'Hara)
PEGGY (Quinn)
PITTY (Aunt)
REBEKAH
ROSEMARY (Butler)
SALLY (Brewton)
SCARLETT O'HARA
SUELLEN
SUKIE
SUSIE (Benteen)
THEODOSIA (Harding)

```
Y T T I P T H E O D O S I A
G P E G E E N N L I L C B O
G C A R R E E N D L U O E H
E N E E L H T A K C T O A E
P A L L I M A C A E I K T T
A N E I L E C E T Y E I R T
N U Y L L A S A I B O E I Y
S A R A H O T T E L R A C S
Y R A M E S O R S I A M E U
M M A M T M O P C O S L R K
M A I Q R N M M A Y I U U I
A R C E A S G A R U M A S E
M I I E I J F M L C L A R E
A E L M I N N I E A L I C E
R E A U T R N E T A I D N I
Y E N A J Z J A T Z A M M E
```

Much of the allure of *Gone With the Wind* is the tempestuous romance between RHETT BUTLER and Scarlett O'Hara. In the sequel, Scarlett finally gives up on recapturing Rhett's heart and decides that she will marry Lord Fenton, who is also known as LUKE. These as well as many other fascinating men can be found in Alexandra Ripley's *Scarlett*; you will find many of them in the puzzle below.

ALEX (Fontaine)
AMOS (Bart)
ASHLEY WILKES
BART (Morland)
BEAU
BILL (Weller)
BRAXTON
BRIAN (O'Hara)
COLUM (O'Hara)
DANNY (Murray)
DAVE (Kennedy)
DESMOND (Grantley)
DR. MEADE
EDWARD (Cooper)
ELIAS
FRANK (Mahoney)
FULWICH
(Bishop) GROSS
HARRY (Connington)
HENRY (Wragg)
JAMES (O'Hara)
JAMIE (O'Hara)
JEROME
JIM (Tarleton)
JOE (Colleton)
JOE (O'Neill)
KERSHAW
KEVIN (O'Connor)
LUKE (Lord Fenton)
MANIGO
MATT (O'Hara)
MILES (Brewton)
PARNELL
PIERRE (Robillard)
PORK
RHETT BUTLER
ROSS (Butler)
(Big) SAM
SAM (Forrest)

SEAMUS (O'Hara)
SEAN (O'Hara)
TED (O'Hara)
TOM (MacMahon)
TONY (Fontaine)

TOWNSEND (Ellinton)
UNCLE HENRY (Hamilton)
WADE
WILL BENTEEN
YANKEES

```
H A R R Y S J D A S O E A E
J C A L E X D O N J E S A D
A O S A M L U K E O H L M A
M L M M D E T O M L M B I E
E U T O N Y S U E E R S D M
S M Y S W A S Y B I I R E R
P O R K I M W A A T A M S D
F E N L L I L N O W T S A O
U D E O L J L K D J O E G J
L A H K B A E E E R W I H E
W W E S E A N E Y R N E H R
I S L B N F R S M A S I E O
C S C L T R A T M A E H V M
H O N L E A P D A N N Y A E
I R U I E N I V E K D T D W
X G P B N K B R A X T O N E
```

HUDSON RIVER ARTISTS

The Hudson River was named after English navigator Henry Hudson, who sailed approximately 150 miles up the river in 1609. This major waterway has been the subject of many paintings. The list below includes the names of 47 artists who've caught the Hudson's magnificence on canvas.

AUDUBON (Victor G.)

BARD (James)

BARTLETT (William H.)

BIERSTADT (Albert)

BROWERE (Albertus)

BROWN (John G.)

CARMIENCKE (Johann H.)

CASILEAR (John)

CHAMBERS (Thomas)

CHAPMAN (Frederic A.)

CHURCH (Frederic E.)

CLAPP (Clinton W.)

COATES (Edmund C.)

COLE (Thomas)

COLMAN (Samuel)

CROPSEY (Jasper F.)

DOUGHTY (Thomas)

DURAND (Asher B.)

EVANS (Jim M.)

FENN (Harry)

FERGUSON (Henry A.)

GERRY (Samuel L.)

GIFFORD (Sanford R.)

GIGNOUX (Régis)

HART (James McDougal)

HART (William)

HASELTINE (William S.)

HAVELL (Robert, Jr.)

HOMER (Winslow)

INNESS (George)

JOHNSON (David)

KENSETT (John F.)

L'ENFANT (Pierre C.)

MARTIN (Homer D.)

MOORE (Charles H.)

MORAN (Edward)

ROBERTSON (Archibald)

RONDEL (Frederick)

ROSSITER (Thomas P.)

SILVA (Francis A.)

SONNTAG (William L.)

SVININ (Pavel P.)

VAN ZANDT (A.)

WALL (William G.)

WARREN (Andrew W.)

WEIR (John F.)

WYANT (Alexander H.)

```
E Q M O X D R O F F I G H A N S E
R L E D N O R E O R J R A H B N O
E X I B L U R M K I O Q S I J A S
W B A N Q G Y O L C H U E Z G V R
O R D T U H C O L E N R L A I E E
R O S S I T E R E U S E T N E H B
B W O C Z Y R E V T O N I T R A M
C N I W O S Y A A U N N N M U I A
E G N L S A Q D H O X G E R R Y H
H O M E R T T E S N E K N O T A C
Y C N N F D C E P V N L B E R W C
D N L F N O O Y S R A E L I S A C
I C B A R T L E T T R N E A U R D
H H R N P L M S T T O W Z D W R W
M U N T I P A P S R M A U A A E Y
D R Y G I G N O U X A B R B N N A
K C R V T F N R I Z O H K A H D N
J H S I L V A C E N A M P A H C T
```

Tender loving care has been taken in constructing this Word Search, which contains 31 6-letter words which all have the letters T, L and C (in any order). None are proper names or plurals. Can you find them all?

YOUR WORD LIST

```
L O L N Y C L A U T C A
O H C T U L C H E L Y H
C A C T Y T T C A L O C
U U L A P C L R T L Q T
S E T L R O E S U U A O
T H U L T T O L E C O L
L C O H E C E I K E L B
S T E S T R Y L A N I O
T I O L N L E L T T A C
E L K Y E L L T A S H I
C G U T I S K L A A A T
L O U C L U C S L C I C
U C I K C U I E A C O A
D T L U M O T E K C O L
```

See word list at end of answer section.

Here's the tale of how the MERMAID met an extra-TERRESTRIAL from another GEOMETRIC plane. It took a LUNGE at her, but missed. It wound up in the TRUNK of a car driven by a VAMPIRE. Okay, ENOUGH is ENOUGH!

AROUSE	LUNGE	PROPONENT	TRUNK
BEHEMOTH	MERMAID	RECEIVE	TYPIFIED
BELOW	NARROWING	ROTISSERIE	UNBURDEN
BONUS	NURSEMAID	SASH	URGE
CUSTODY	OPULENT	SLEIGHT	VAMPIRE
DEPOSITION	PODIUM	TERRESTRIAL	WAXEN
DETRACTED	PRODUCE	TICKER	WHEREFORE
DREARIER			
EMULSION			
ENOUGH			
EQUALED			
FAUCET			
FLICKER			
GEOMETRIC			
GREBE			
HURRICANE			
INTO			
KNEEL			
LABORED			
LARD			

The 25 foods listed below all have one thing in common: they make a lot of noise when you eat them! See if you can locate all of these crunchy foods hidden in the diagram below. We've circled PICKLE to help you get started.

```
P O T A T O C H I P E S C T
R L U A L M O N D Z P U U M
C D N E P A N S R E G N I G
C R L L O P E C A N T F A I
E Y A K K N L N C S U L N Q
L C W C B C U E E R O O R T
E E Y I K T I H O N R W O U
R R Z P A E C T A D P E C N
Y E A T U R R R S E S R P L
Q A Z D E L G C L D N S O I
E L T T I R B T U N A E P Z
T S A O T S P A Q O E E C A
F W Q L G K H C M E B D R R
T O R R A C R O U T O N H B
```

ALMOND

APPLE

BEAN SPROUT

BRAZIL NUT

BREADSTICK

CARROT

CELERY

CRACKER

CROUTON

DRY CEREAL

GINGER SNAP

GRANOLA

PEANUT

PEANUT BRITTLE

PECAN

PICKLE

POPCORN

POTATO CHIP

PRETZEL

RADISH

SUNFLOWER SEED

TACO

TOAST

WALNUT

WATER CHESTNUT

TWO-WHEELER ─────────────── 37

The word "bicycle" comes from the Latin word *bis* meaning "twice" and the Greek word *kyklos* meaning "circle." Although the basic principle of the bicycle has remained unchanged since 1885, modern refinements such as multiple GEARS and the DERAILLEUR have greatly improved cycling's pleasure.

ASHTABULA
  CRANK
AXLE
BRAKES
CABLE
CAGE
CARRIER
CHAIN
CHANGER
CONTROL
CROWN
DERAILLEUR
FORK
FRAME
FREEWHEEL
GEARS
GUARD
HANDLEBAR
HUBS
LEVER
LIGHT
LOCK
LUGS
PEDAL
PLUG
POST
PUMP
QUICK RELEASE

RIMS
SEAT
SHOE
SPOKE

SPROCKET
STEM
TIRE
VALVE

```
G B F R E E W H E E L S T A
O R C P E W B S V K O N S R
Q G M E T S P P R S R H O Q
S U N W O R C O E T T A S U
P L I K O E F K S A N N P J
E P L C L I A E B T O D L C
R J K O K R X U E U C L H H
I E R L B R L X G V D E U A
T A E S R A E G A E L B R N
D Y C T C C V L C L S A A G
S V H R H C E S E B A R V E
E M A R F G R G U A R D G R
C N I M R B I U S C S X E V
K L N R U E L L I A R E D P
```

45

The *piñata* continues to be a popular party toy and decoration, especially for children during the holiday season. The children are blindfolded and given sticks so they can hit the *piñata*, which is hung overhead. When it's smashed open, all kinds of candies and toys tumble to the ground. Hidden below are 25 items used to make this colorful toy.

AWL
BOWL
BRISTOL BOARD
CARBON PAPER
CLOTHESPIN
CORD
GIFT WRAP
GLUE
HAMMER
HOOK
KNIFE
NAIL
NEWSPAPER
PENCIL
PLASTER OF PARIS
ROPE
SCISSORS
SCREWDRIVER
SCREW-EYE
SODA BOTTLE
SPOON
TAPE
TISSUE PAPER
TRACING PAPER
WATER

```
T I S S U E P A P E R L E R
A M O I E A W P J B Z Q F E
L O C R E L I C N E P D N V
N S P A R W T F I G R D I I
E C O P R D Y T H A L Q P R
O R N F R B N O O P S U S D
L E B O W L O B O B V H E W
E W C R H A L N K C A O H E
F E I E Z O T L P M Z D T R
I Y A T T L C E M A E A O C
N E W S P A P E R V P Y L S
K L I A N J R L S E O E C Z
Q R E L S C I S S O R S R T
B R E P A P G N I C A R T G
```

Do you have any stained glass sun-catchers hanging in your kitchen windows? They are beautiful to look at and aren't difficult to make at home. All you need is a how-to book and the items listed below.

ACID BRUSH

ANTIQUE (glass)

BATTEN STRIPS

CATHEDRAL (glass)

COPPER FOIL

FELT

FILE

FLUX

GLASS CUTTER

GLUE

HAMMER

IRON (soldering)

KEROSENE

LEAD CAME

PAPER

PLIERS

POLISH

RAGS

RHEOSTAT

ROLLER

RULER

SAFETY GOGGLES

SEEDY (glass)

SOLDER

STRETCHER (came)

TEMPLATE

TIPS (soldering)

TRANSLUCENT (glass)

WET STONE

WIRE

```
G A C I D B R U S H S R L B
S T O L R E L L O R T P S A
R E P A P G L U E A N E I T
H M P J A N T I Q U E O Y T
E P E O C H L E A D C A M E
O L R R A P S N Y L U R N N
S A F E T Y G O G G L E S S
T T O M H R A T E K S M F T
A E I F E C R S W O N M I R
T Z L D D R T T R I A A L I
R U L E R J I E L H R H E P
X O H W A Q K W R E T O J S
S H S I L O P A Q T F I N E
F E P R E T T U C S S A L G
```

From "The Marshal of Gunsight Pass" to "The Young Riders," the Old West setting has given rise to many different shows. James ARNESS was in "Gunsmoke" for 20 seasons. "Bonanza" was on the air for 14 seasons. Here are 36 actors who have played cowboys on television.

1. ARNESS (James)
2. AUTRY (Gene)
3. BARRY (Gene)
4. BLOCKER (Dan)
5. BOND (Ward)
6. BOYD (William)
7. BRAND (Neville)
8. BRENNAN (Walter)
9. BROLIN (Josh)
10. CASE (Allen)
11. CONNORS (Chuck)
12. CULP (Robert)
13. DEAN (Eddie)
14. DUEL (Peter)
15. EASTWOOD (Clint)
16. ELAM (Jack)
17. FULLER (Robert)
18. GARNER (James)
19. GREENE (Lorne)
20. HARTMAN (David)
21. HORSLEY (Lee)
22. HUNTER (Jeffrey)
23. HUTCHINS (Will)
24. KELLY (Jack)
25. LANDON (Michael)
26. LA RUE (Lash)
27. LONG (Richard)
28. MADISON (Guy)
29. MCQUEEN (Steve)
30. MILLER (Ty)
31. MOORE (Clayton)
32. PYLE (Denver)
33. RENALDO (Duncan)
34. ROBERTSON (Dale)
35. ROGERS (Roy)
36. WARD (Larry)

```
V K S N I H C T U H R D C B
C L W R B M C Q U E E N R R
R R B R O L L R P G T E L O
W E A R E N R A G L N L Y B
C N L U O W N J L N U O E E
D A D L A L K O A A H C L R
O L A R U E I N C M N Y S T
O D D R T F D N O B P D R S
W O L O R G A O Q S R L O O
T Y O G Y M R E L L I M H N
S B R E T E K E L L Y D A M
A T A R N E S S E J L E A C
E R A S A Z L A Q N D L L M
C H D Y O B L O C K E R T C
```

See television shows at end of answer section.

In the old West a working cowboy's life was difficult. His work was hard and often dangerous. As rugged as his lot was, there were many interesting and beautiful things for him to see.

BARN

CAMPFIRE

CHAPARRAL

CHAPS

CORRAL

COWBOYS

COYOTES

DOGIE

DROVERS

FENCE

FOAL

GRASS

HACIENDA

HERD

HORSES

LARIAT

LIVESTOCK

LONGHORNS

MULES

PASTURE

PLAINS

PONIES

PRAIRIE

RANCHERO

SADDLE

SILO

STABLE

WAGON

WELL

WOLF

```
K V L W K W S Q V G Q J N S
P Q H A C S Q Y R H E R D A
X E I G O D E A O C A O Q D
C O Y O T E S I A B R K O D
J L K N S S L M N E W L Q L
Q W A X E J P W H O I O T E
A L K R V F E C L S P N C X
S D A Z I L N F J K L G E S
S R N R L A R R A P A H C T
L C E E R U T S A P I O N A
I A H V I O L K W Q N R E B
A D O A O C C Z M R S N F L
R L J F P R A I R I E S Z E
T M U L E S D H O R S E S Q
```

SOUTHERN PLANTATIONS ──────────

If you've ever been to the beautiful state of Virginia, you may have visited MOUNT VERNON, the magnificent home of George Washington, or ASHLAWN, the home of the fifth U.S. President, James Monroe. Find these and 36 other plantation houses of the Old South below. State locations are in parentheses (but not in the diagram).

ASHLAND (KY)

ASHLAWN (VA)

BEAUVOIR (MS)

BELLE MEADE (Mansion, TN)

BERKELEY (VA)

BOONE (Hall, SC)

CARTER'S GROVE (VA)

CRAGFONT (TN)

DESTREHAN (Plantation Manor House, LA)

DRAYTON (Hall, SC)

DUNLEITH (MS)

FARMINGTON (KY)

FEDERAL HILL (KY)

GAINESWOOD (AL)

GUNSTON (Hall, VA)

HAMPTON (SC)

HERMITAGE (The; TN)

HOFWYL-BROADFIELD (Plantation, GA)

HOPE (Plantation, NC)

HOUMAS (House Plantation, LA)

KENMORE (VA)

LONGWOOD (MS)

MAGNOLIA (SC)

MELROSE (MS)

MIDDLETON (Place, SC)

MONTICELLO (VA)

MOUNT VERNON (VA)

OAK HILL (GA)

PEBBLE HILL (Plantation, GA)

POPLAR GROVE (NC)

ROSEDOWN (Plantation and Gardens, LA)

ROSE HILL (State Park, SC)

SAN FRANCISCO (Plantation House, LA)

SHERWOOD FOREST (VA)

SHIRLEY (VA)

SOMERSET (Place, NC)

STRATFORD (Hall, VA)

WOODLAWN (VA)

```
N P M E L R O S E D O W N S O M K D
O E A Q G N A N R H N F H H L E H L
T B G W H O K Q O H O I P O L V O B
E B N D J T H N K T R P N U E O F N
L L O E N Y I V O L P G E M C R W T
D E L S O A L E E T W M G A I G Y S
D H I T T R L Y L O G Y A S T S L E
I I A R S D I H O N E N T H N R B R
M L C E N X H D S L U Z I T O E R O
S L R H U B L W E A R D M M M T O F
T I A A G A A K E N M O R E R R A D
R H G N W Q R I O V U A E B Q A D O
A E F N G E E D N W A L H S A C F O
T S O Q B E D A E M E L L E B Q I W
F O N O N R E V T N U O M C O O E R
O R T S A N F R A N C I S C O P L E
R C P O P L A R G R O V E L N H D H
D O O W S E N I A G T E S R E M O S
```

At the XXV Olympiad in Barcelona, Spain (July–August 1992), a total of 788 gold, silver, and bronze medals were awarded to athletes from 64 countries out of 176 countries represented. The Unified Team (a coalition of former republics of the Soviet Union) led the winners with 112 medals, followed by the USA with 108 medals. The 31 countries listed each won at least 3 medals. The number in parentheses after each name tells how many that country earned.

```
C A N A D A I L A R T S U A
Z F B U L G A R I A Y W N B
E U R Q S C K N O A C I A J
C L I A Z P X E W M H D P L
H J T K N L A R N C A E A S
O P A A D C O I D Y M N J D
S W I I X N E N N N A M I N
L S N R Y T A C I A M A J A
O W O E H L U L E M J R G L
V E B G N P A R A R X K V R
A D J I Q E O T Z E Y T I E
K E F N R K B L I G Z R O H
I N D O N E S I A Q A W V T
A L K Y E K R U T N T Z E E
Q S H U N G A R Y P D X J N
V W U M A E T D E I F I N U
```

AUSTRALIA (27)
BRITAIN (20)
BULGARIA (16)
CANADA (18)
CHINA (54)
CUBA (31)
CZECHO-
 SLOVAKIA (7)
DENMARK (6)
FINLAND (5)
FRANCE (29)
GERMANY (82)
HUNGARY (30)
INDONESIA (5)
IRAN (3)
ITALY (19)
JAMAICA (4)
JAPAN (22)
KENYA (8)
NETHERLANDS (15)
NEW ZEALAND (10)
NIGERIA (4)
N. KOREA (9)
NORWAY (7)
POLAND (19)
ROMANIA (18)
S. KOREA (29)
SPAIN (22)
SWEDEN (12)
TURKEY (6)
UNIFIED TEAM (112)
USA (108)

cod

Can you find the names of 23 types of sporting events held during the Summer Olympics hidden in the diagram below?

ARCHERY
BASEBALL
BASKETBALL
BOXING
CANOEING
CYCLING
EQUESTRIAN
(events)
FENCING
GYMNASTICS
HANDBALL
HOCKEY (field)
JUDO
PENTATHLON
ROWING
SHOOTING
SOCCER
SWIMMING
TENNIS
TRACK AND FIELD
VOLLEYBALL
WEIGHTLIFTING
WRESTLING
YACHTING

```
G E Q V O L L E Y B A L L J A
A Y H I Z L D G A G K T U B H
R G M Q C A Q S N N X D R O C
C N H N Y B K R W I O H C X R
H I A K A E R T J L M K P I K
E T W S T S X E T C E M E N W
R F D B C A T E C Y K Q I G R
Y I A Y G B N I A C U C G W E
L L A B D N A H C E O W N R S
L T H W I C I E S S X S I L T
K H A S G N I T O O H S E D L
A G N I W O R I H W N D O E I
C I B L C I Y M G C I U N L N
P E N T A T H L O N A J A C G
I W L N G N I C N E F Y C L I
B Q D L E I F D N A K C A R T
```

53

Scan the grid in all directions for 34 familiar five-letter words, arranged in pairs. Each word in a pair crosses its partner through the center letter, forming either a "+" or an "x" shape. One pair has been circled to start you off.

YOUR WORD LIST

```
E V A F Y X L R C T O H B
R T L E H E J C O L W P E
C H A R M C L A R O M R K
Y O R A B A S E A I S Z D
I L M U I L L T L M M N A
Y M R M G P W B L L E P S
A L F U A A E A E R L N I
Y R L Q C M Z A T E L R D
C L O U T E S E C H I L L
Y U U U D E T M D E R W O
H S T R F L A R E A D Y N
M O B E N T I V L D E H P
R C J T R A R Y G Y O S A
```

See word list at end of answer section.

54

Solve this puzzle by forming a chain of circled words in which the last letter of one word is the first letter of the next. The number in parentheses tells you the length of the word you're looking for. We have provided FILE to start you off.

FILE _____ (4)	_____ (5)	_____ (5)
E _____ (4)	_____ (4)	_____ (4)
_____ (4)	_____ (4)	_____ (5)
_____ (5)	_____ (4)	_____ (5)
_____ (5)	_____ (4)	_____ (6)
_____ (4)		
_____ (5)		
_____ (5)		
_____ (7)		
_____ (6)		
_____ (4)		
_____ (5)		
_____ (4)		
_____ (6)		
_____ (9)		
_____ (5)		
_____ (5)		
_____ (4)		
_____ (6)		
_____ (5)		
_____ (4)		
_____ (4)		
_____ (6)		
_____ (5)		
_____ (5)		
_____ (5)		
_____ (4)		
_____ (4)		
_____ (4)		

```
T F I R D M L L G R L L A H
H Y H N L I L K K I S Y C G
U G L W E B O M M C S T R L
S W M S I M R I R L E L I F
S O W W Y A T A Z Z M G L M
G R U A O Y M H N Y B A I E
M Q R R S G N E T T I K R L
W P P M A R E S O Z S N Z D
S Q N M L E E Q P W Q A Z H
S J Q O A D D E R R O R U S
O B H T A L S G C I A L Z A
B Z R I Z O C I T N A I Z U
M U L O Y F E I R G A B N Q
E T Z N O M I N A T E D P S
```

See word list at end of answer section.

RECIPE: SHRIMP AND MUSHROOMS

This is an especially good recipe for calorie counters. When served with marinated cucumbers and icy cold, fresh pineapple for dessert, it will make four servings of 220 calories each. All the words in the list are taken directly from the recipe and are hidden in the grid on the opposite page.

BEEF	EACH	MUSHROOMS	SPOON
BROTH	GINGER	OUNCES	STIR
BUTTER	HEAT	OVER	TABLESPOON
CANS	HOT	PEPPER	TEASPOON
CELERY	INTO	RICE	TENDER
CHOPPED	LARGE	SERVING	THICKENS
COOK	MELT	SHRIMP	THROUGH
CORNSTARCH	MINUTES	SKILLET	UNTIL
CUPS	MIX	SLICED	WATER
DRAINED	MIXTURE	SOY SAUCE	

Shrimp and Mushrooms

2 tablespoons butter
2 cups chopped celery
1 can (6 ounces) sliced
  mushrooms, drained
1 tablespoon soy sauce
1 tablespoon ginger
⅛ teaspoon pepper

1 tablespoon cornstarch
1 tablespoon water
½ cup beef broth
2 cans (4½ ounces each) shrimp,
  rinsed and drained
2 cups hot cooked rice

Melt butter in large skillet. Cook and stir celery, mushrooms, soy sauce, ginger and pepper until celery is tender, about 5 minutes. Mix cornstarch and water. Stir cornstarch and broth into celery and mushrooms. Cook, stirring frequently, until mixture thickens. Stir in shrimp, heat through. Spoon each serving over ½ cup of rice. Serves four.

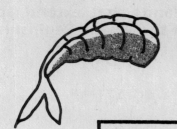

```
N O O P S A E T E L L I K S
D S V B K N O B R O T H E M
Y E E E U H E I E A E R A O
R R C L R T C K B E U A U O
E V O I H E T L C T F N C R
L I O T L C E E X I C A E H
E N K N U S R I R E H S E S
C G C U P S M A S E H T R U
U C R O S I P R T R D G T M
A A O A N N E E I S I N A E
S N X U L T P M R N N A E L
Y S T I A O P H G U O R H T
O E H W M R E E T S P O O N
S D E N I A R D E P P O H C
```

The Aleutian Islands are a chain of volcanic islands that extend approximately 1200 miles westward from the tip of the Alaska Peninsula. Among them are the 27 that appear below.

```
U T T A P I K A N K I S K A
U N L S U O K A N A G A O C
N B I E A V J E N L G V P R
G U A M A T I G N A K A R N
A D U I A R K H L M S O I Y
K S L S P K R A N C M K D U
S M T O G A S Y A H T X L K
A C A P E K Y R U I A K U N
L O T O A G A U S T K N B G
A K K C L T A E N K T H R T
N C U H A G L A V A K A A L
U I M N R T U M G M S G G T
C H A O T Y G U M N A K U A
A G L I C H E R B E R T A N
A K L T O G S E G U A M L O
```

AGATTU
AKUN
AMATIGNAK
AMCHITKA
AMLIA
AMUKTA
ATKA
ATTU
BULDIR
HERBERT
KAGALASKA
KANAGA
KAVALGA
KISKA
LITTLE SITKIN
NAGAI
RAT
SANAK
SEGUAM
SEGULA
SEMISOPOCHNOI
TANAGA
UMNAK
UNALASKA
UNGA
UNIMAK
YUNASKA

William Seward purchased Alaska from the Russians in 1867 at the cost of two cents an acre. Two years later 33,000 newcomers had moved into that vast wilderness. The Gold Rush of 1898 doubled the population and led to the coining of new words and phrases unique to Alaskan life.

BANANA BELT

BANYA

BERM

BLACK DIAMOND

BREAKUP

BURN

BUSH

CABIN FEVER

CHUCK

DOG MUSHER

FISH CAMP

FREEZE-UP

HAUL ROAD

ICE BRIDGE

IGLOO

IRON DOG
  (snowmobile)

KUPIAK (coffee)

KUSPUK (Inuit dress)

MUSKEG

PARKA

RUFF

SNOW-GO
  (snowmobile)

STACK ROBBER
  (stove device)

STATESIDE

TAKU WIND

TILLICUM (friend)

TOOLIES
  (remote areas)

TYEE (salmon)

UTILIDOR
  (insulated box)

WANIGAN
  (portable building)

```
Z A Y N A B K K A I P U K J
K G G E K S U M C H U C K B
U T I L I D O R T H K Q I H
P L C L H Z S T N Y A C R I
S E M F C A B I N F E V E R
U B R R I E U L W B R E B O
K A E E H S D L R P B P B N
T N B E H N H I R H A K O D
O A L Z L S D C S O Q R R O
O N K E R G U U A E A N K G
L A Q U E Z B M H M T D C A
I B F P W O O L G I P A A L
E F W A N I G A N O Z Q T W
S N O G W O N S Z C D L S S
N D N O M A I D K C A L B T
```

When the circus comes to town, some of the most popular attractions under the big top are the trapeze artists. Below you'll find the first verse of the song "The Daring Young Man on the Flying Trapeze," with words by George Leybourne. Words grouped together will be found hidden together in the diagram.

```
A G T G I R L S C V H L
A W R Z S C I E O E L O
D T A E H V H M F L I V
E H P Y A T L L E W N E
N E E Z N T I N A C E H
I A Z O D E E V S F W E
O I E R S A Z S E L I R
L R Z A O Y R S T Y T U
R H E J M N I I O I H G
U L K D E H M H N N T I
P L N B T H R O U G H F
N A M G N U O Y B L E Z
```

He flies
through
the air
with the
greatest
of ease,
This
daring
young man
on the
flying
trapeze;
His
figure
is handsome,
all
girls
he can
please,
And my
love he
purloined
her
away!

No circus would be complete without its trapeze artists, doing the impossible "with the greatest of ease." But the originator of that art form is more famous for something else. Solve the puzzle to find out why.

The
original
"Daring
Young
Man on
the Flying
Trapeze"
appeared
in Paris
in eighteen
fifty-
nine.
Others
had hung
from
bars
but he
was the
first
to swing
from
trapeze
to trapeze.
But
he is
best
known
today

for the
tight
costume
he wore.

His name
was
Jules
Léotard.

```
G J O H L Z Y T U B R I Y F
G N U H D A H H F G S U T I
E N U L D G N G N M R R F R
R H I O E E N I N P A R I S
O T T Y Y S W T G P B N F T
W Z S R L S C A E I E Z O N
E D R J O F B Z S I R K W N
H I E T T F E I G F R O M L
Q Y H R R P S H I S N A M E
K E T R A X T J T K T M T O
A Z O R P E M U T S O C H T
B U T H E C P Y R R A B R A
Z O I N Z O I P F L U W V R
T K S I E H C D A R I N G D
```

Velvet is one of the silk weaves developed on the ancient shuttle looms of China. India has produced velvet from remote times, often richly embroidered and used to cover the furniture of royalty. The word VELVET is listed below in 25 different languages.

```
O F H U L T I B A R S O N Y
V L I A U Q M N I Q L U F T
E U Q E F I D A K R U L I E
L W J G T I Z F S A O M N R
O E S A M E T A Z Y A O U C
U E C H I A M E E S V D D I
D L I A Z E H L K A S U E O
O U Q A T I F A L M R L L P
R U U T H I D O M M U E E E
U B I L J I F F L E O V B L
L J O L F G H E R T L P I O
E D S A Z V N H A X E I P L
V E L L U T O I N G V I Z I
O V E L V E T A H K R A B O
```

AKSAMIT (Polish)
BÁRKHAT (Russian)
BÁRSONY
   (Hungarian)
BELEDU (Indonesian)
BIROODO
   (Japanese)
CATIFEA (Romanian)
FLOJL (Danish)
FLOYEL (Norwegian)
FLUWEEL (Dutch)
KADIFA (Serbo-
   Croatian)
KADIFE (Turkish)
KETIFAH (Hebrew)
MAHAMELI
   (Swahili)
QATIFA (Arabic)
SAMET (Czech,
   Yiddish)
SAMETTI (Finnish)
SAMMET (Swedish)
SAMT (German)
TERCIOPELO
   (Spanish)
VELLUTO (Italian)
VELOU'DO (Greek)
VELOURS (French)
VELUDO
   (Portuguese)
VELURO (Esperanto)
VELVET (English)

The titles of many films have featured generals, admirals, and lieutenants, but captains seem to be the moviemakers' favorite. We have listed below the names of 28 captains in movie titles. You'll be first-rank brass when you have found them all.

AFRICA
AMERICA
APACHE
BLOOD
BOYCOTT
CAREY
CAUTION
CHINA
EDDIE
FABIAN
FALCON
FURY
JANUARY
JOHN SMITH
KIDD
KRONOS
LIGHTFOOT
MARVEL
MEPHISTO
MIDNIGHT
NEMO
NEWMAN M.D.
SCARLETT
SINBAD
SIROCCO
THUNDER
TUGBOAT ANNIE
VIDEO

```
T W Z D D I K R O N O S A Q
T H U N D E R M N W C F K V
R F Q O E V I M M A R V E L
W X O D I D V D R I S H I A
Z L D D N X M E C I C G M S
B I E I N N Y A R A H E C Z
E O G V A T Q O P T R A Q O
Z H Y M T Y C A F I R V T D
T N W C A C R O C L Y S D F
Q E C X O W O A E R I A A A
N M D N B T Z T U H B B N L
V O V F G K T F P N I X I C
N O I T U A C E I A A Z H O
Z S V H T I M S N H O J C N
```

There is no free lunch in this puzzle, but you have free REIN to find the 36 words that form a familiar word or phrase when preceded by the word "free."

AGENT	FALL	GOLD
ALONGSIDE SHIP	FLIGHT	HANDED
BOARD	FLOATING	HEARTED
BORN	FOR-ALL	HOLD
ENTERPRISE	FORM	KICK
		LANCE
		LOVE
		MARKET
		MASON
		ON BOARD
		PORT
		REIN
		RIDE
		SILVER
		SOIL
		SPOKEN
		STANDING
		STONE
		SWIMMING
		THINKER
		THROW
		TRADE
		VERSE
		WAY
		WHEEL
		WILL

```
R R M E C N A L S P O K E N
E E Z A Q U L W U J N Y A W
S V I L R E N O T S B L O Y
H L L N E K T R E V O L M O
C I L H S H E H D N A X R S
W S W A I W H T G D R A O B
D O E N R C I S N I D I F E
E P K S P O I M D B L A L B
T E O Z R D F E M A E F O M
R E S R E V S L T I E R A A
A K O S T E G N I D N A T S
E C H A N D E D A L L G I O
H I U H E G E R N O M O N N
P K L L A F T G S H V E G W
```

LOOSE LETTERS ———————————————— 55

To solve, remove one letter from each word in the list to form a shorter word without changing the order of the letters. Write the "loose" letter on the dash, and look for the new word in the diagram. The loose letters, read down, will reveal a proverb. We've done the first one for you as an example.

SHALLOW   H
CAUSED   ___
LINENS   ___
GLANDS   ___
BEAKED   ___
LODGER   ___
MOTHER   ___
BOARDER   ___
MONKEY   ___
EMOTES   ___
CURSED   ___
PHEASANT   ___
HURRAY   ___
FRIGHT   ___
PRIDES   ___
BRIDGE   ___
WEAKER   ___
PAUNCH   ___
RANGER   ___
SHARES   ___
DESSERT   ___
SWINGS   ___
SCRAPE   ___
CREATED   ___
COVERT   ___

```
D E T A R C J S E T O M
T S Q Z Q R A G E R M B
S I C M Z L L S T S C L
E N M R L J G F E E O J
I G B O A I R Z G D V F
R S W T N P N D G V E I
P E H H D E I E Q W R G
U Y D E S R Y K S H W H
N Z E R Q P E A S A N T
C G R L O Z Y B K R H C
H D U R K B D E S E R T
P R C W H U R R Y S P N
```

See word list at end of answer section.

65

THE POWERS THAT BE

The Congress of the United States is comprised of the Senate and the House of Representatives. If you're interested in a career in politics, the only requirements are that you are a US citizen, and are at least 30 years old to be a senator or 25 to be a representative. This puzzle lists 44 international legislative and religious bodies. Can you find them all?

ASSEMBLY

BENCH (law court)

BOARD

BUNDESRAT (German legislature)

CABINET

CAPUT (English university council)

CHAMBER

COMITIA (Roman legislature)

COMMITTEE

CONGRESS

CONSISTORY (council)

CORTES (Portuguese legislature)

COUNCIL

COURT

CURIA (papal legislature)

DAIL EIREANN (Irish legislature)

DIET (legislative assembly)

DIRECTOIRE (French executive body)

DIRECTORY

DIVAN (royal Oriental council)

DUMA (Russian parliament)

FOLKESTING (Danish parliament)

HOUSE

JUNTA (Spanish legislature)

LANDSTING (Danish parliament)

LEGISLATURE

PARLIAMENT

PRESBYTER (ecclesiastical council)

REICHSRAT (German legislature)

REICHSTAG (German parliament)

RIGSDAG (Danish parliament)

RIKSDAG (Swedish parliament)

SANHEDRIN (Jewish council)

SENATE

SENATUS (senate)

SOVIET (Russian council)

STORTING (Norwegian parliament)

SYNDICATE (council)

SYNOD (ecclesiastical council)

TRIBUNAL (court)

VESTRY (Anglican administration)

WITAN (Anglo-Saxon council)

WITENAGEMOT (Anglo-Saxon parliament)

ZEMSTVO (Russian legislature)

```
D A I L E I R E A N N C G B E S T
B C M S E E T T I M M O C L A T P
R A V E D G K E B E I R C U R I A
A B E N C H I U S E F T H C C M R
D I V A N S N S T O Z E A O H S L
G N I T S D N A L E S S M U P S I
C E K U E A N K M A Y I B N A E A
Y T L S M E E S N V T C E C S R M
R E R U S S T H O I S U R I S G E
O A D U T V E D A X Y W R L E N N
T R I I O D W I T E N A G E M O T
S I N V R C N R N R D R A O B C A
I G C I T E H E T E I V O S L T R
S S N U I D C C N Y C B H M Y S S
N D P D N T V T E A A W U O Y S H
O A N O G M E O O O T A T N U J C
C G A T S H C I E R E I O L A S I
M V E S T R Y R D T Y D W G I L E
Y R E T Y B S E R P G A D S K I R
```

In RINGER, the official marbles tournament game, shooters at the edge of a 10-foot ring try to knock out 13 marbles arranged in the center. The first to score 7 hits wins. Listed below are 30 games played with these colorful glass, metal, stone, or clay objects.

ABACUS

BIG RING

BOSS-OUT

BOXIES

CHASIES

CIRCLE

CORONA

DA BAWH JI

DICIES

FOOTBALL

HO-GO

HOLILAKES

HUNDREDS

IMMIE

LAG

MILKIE

NUCKS

PERSIAN

PINBALL

POTSIES

PUGGY

PUREES

PYRAMIDS

RINGER

ROCKIES

SKELLY

SPANNING

SPINNER

STICKER

WALL

```
P R T W J G N I R G I B O S
H E L C R I C E B O X I E S
O K R H I Q G O C R G I Q E
L C A S U N S E I K C O R E
I I J Q I S S P W I J O N R
L T Z R O A Y E D W G O S U
A S L U A R N R P O Q P P P
K M T D A B A W H J I L A L
E I M M I Y A U A N E E N L
S P I I L Z N C N L L V N A
N D U L L D I E U Q L L I B
S U E G R K R O H S M A N T
D K C E G P I N B A L L G O
S M D K N Y S E I S T O P O
L S E I S A H C O R O N A F
```

It was at Covent Garden, London's former produce and flower market, that Eliza Doolittle, in the musical *My Fair Lady*, hawked her bouquets. The district still houses the National Gallery, several famous churches, and the Royal Opera House, but its thoroughfares are now lined with rows of chic boutiques. Stroll through the diagram to locate 36 streets of Covent Garden.

ADELAIDE	RUSSELL	TOWER
AGAR	SHELTON	WEST
ARNE	STUKELEY	WILD
BEDFORD	TAVISTOCK	WILLIAM IV
BETTERTON		
BOW		
BURLEIGH		
CATHERINE		
CRANBOURN		
DRYDEN		
EARLHAM		
ENDELL		
EXETER		
FLORAL		
GARRICK		
HENRIETTA		
JAMES		
KEAN		
KEELEY		
KEMBLE		
KING		
LANGLEY		
MACKLIN		
MERCER		
NEAL		
NEWTON		
PARKER		
ROSE		

```
T B E D F O R D F H N X K D
S L O K I N G L N E W C W M
E Y C W E S O R W N I Q E A
W M A L C R H T K R L N K H
I B T D A R O E R I D C A L
L U H L E N E A L E O V Y R
L R E C X L G M L T T B E A
I L R F E A A L S T O T L E
A E I Y Q C E I E A G N E L
M I N N K S V N D Y A J K B
I G E L S A R E T E X E U M
V H I U T A R E K R A P T E
L N R E W O T M J A M E S K
D R Y D E N R U O B N A R C
```

If you IMMERSE yourself in your solving, we think you'll have no problem finding the 48 words of five or more letters hidden in the diagram below. Why not give it a WHIRL?

ADORN   CIVIL   GRACE   MAMMAL

AFFORD   CREED   GROWTH   MAMMOTH

BIRCH   FARCE   HURRAH   MARCH

CANOE   FLEET   IMMERSE   MEANDER

CAUCUS   FLUTE   KNEEL   MERIT

CHAIR   FRESH   LAUGH   MOTTO

CHEST   FRUIT   LUMBER   NORTH

ORIOLE

OTHER

PIECE

PRUNE

RODEO

ROOST

RURAL

SHOVE

SIMMER

TIMBER

TOAST

TRAIL

UNCLE

UTTER

VAULT

VELVET

VOUCH

WHIRL

WREST

WRONG

```
T G P C H A I R H T W O R G
M L R C C A U C U S S E V N
H G U A L N O T R O D E O O
E O N A C W T F R N Q D R R
V V E L V E T R A L R I H W
O G E U R I O E H R O O S T
H T O M M A M M A L C M D O
S S H B A H L M E H A E F A
F L E E T R P I E C E R L S
B R N R R P C S V R U I U T
D R O F F A T H C I S T T R
K N E E L I A R T B C E E T
```

Giacomo PUCCINI is celebrated for his lyric style and expressive melodies, as shown in his operas *La Bohème, Tosca, Madama Butterfly* and *Turandot*. Face the music and find PUCCINI and 31 other notable Italian composers hidden below.

ALBINONI (Tomaso)
BASSANO (Giovanni)
BELLINI (Vincenzo)
BERIO (Luciano)
BERTOLI (Giovanni)
BOCCHERINI (Luigi)
BOITO (Arrigo)
BOTTESINI (Giovanni)
CALLACE (Raffaele)
DONIZETTI (Gaetano)
FONTATA (Giovanni)
GUIDETTI (Giovanni)
LANDI (Stefano)
LAPPI (Pietro)
LEONI (Franco)
MARCELLO (Benedetto)
MARINI (Biagio)
NENNA (Pomponio)
NONO (Luigi)
PAGANINI (Niccolò)
PALESTRINA (Giovanni)
PERI (Jacopo)

PICCINI (Nicolà)
PORPORA (Nicolo)
PUCCINI (Giacomo)
ROSSINI (Gioacchino)
SALIERI (Antonio)

SCARLATTI (Domenico)
SPONTINI (Gaspare)
TARTINI (Giuseppe)
VERDI (Giuseppe)
VIVALDI (Antonio)

```
P A L E S T R I N A I L I T
A T A T N O F M L B E T A I
G I P B A S S A N O N R I N
A T P O R P O R A E T O D O
N T I R O S S I N I E R R N
I E C D R O C N N C E O E I
N Z C O N T A I A V N T V B
I I I L I A R L N O A I S L
S N N L B E L L N O V O A A
E O I E H A A E M A E B L S
T D R C C U T B L I P L I A
T I C R C A T D A N C E E G
O O L A G U I D E T T I R N
B L I M P S P O N T I N I I
```

HOLD THAT TIGER! ——————————— 61

There's a tiger lurking among the letters in the diagram below. It looks as though there's a whole pack of them, but only *one* is hiding. Can you spot it?

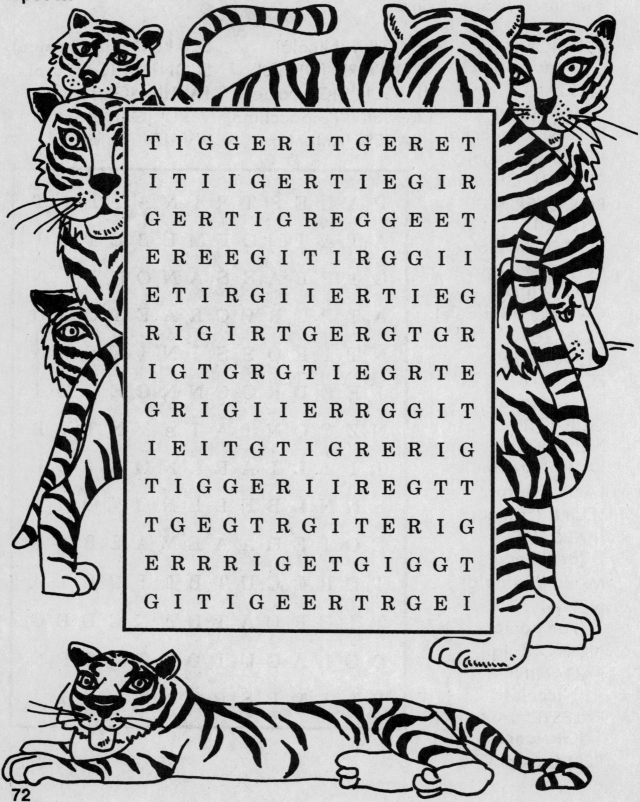

```
T I G G E R I T G E R E T
I T I I G E R T I E G I R
G E R T I G R E G G E E T
E R E E G I T I R G G I I
E T I R G I I E R T I E G
R I G I R T G E R G T G R
I G T G R G T I E G R T E
G R I G I I E R R G G I T
I E I T G T I G R E R I G
T I G G E R I I R E G T T
T G E G T R G I T E R I G
E R R R I G E T G I G G T
G I T I G E E R T R G E I
```

72

Irishman Cormac McCarthy built Blarney Castle in the 15th century. It has walls eighteen feet thick and is home to the nearly inaccessible Blarney Stone. Solve the puzzle below and learn about this popular legend.

An old
Irish
legend
has it
that
you will
receive
the gift
of eloquence
if you
kiss
the famous
Blarney
Stone.
The stone
is located
near
the top
of the
southernmost
wall of
Blarney
Castle.
The castle

is about
four
miles

from
Cork,
Ireland.

```
L L I W U O Y E N R A L B
B G C R L T H C E T M N I
C T A S M T H N H C O R K
M E S T F I G E H T I X I
N I T O H A C U S S T R S
D Y L N M A N Q H T U U S
N E E E S N T O B D O Y T
E I T T S F R L L M B N H
G R L A O F A E A D A V E
E E U L C R R F H A S I T
L L L O N O E O H T I C O
H A J E F H L N M T U Q P
W N Y C T N G S I F Y O U
B D Q T R E C E I V E J S
```

Fahrenheit 451 is a novel by sci-fi master Ray Bradbury. It is also the temperature at which book paper catches fire and burns. See if you can find the 5-digit combinations hidden in the diagram below.

00531	02351	04357	26817
00589	02711	04778	26857
01315	03198	25191	27571
01935	03987	25519	27817
			28159
			28891
			29531
			29731
			40518
			40878
			41911
			41977
			42139
			42879
			43157
			43778
			44973
			44989
			65311
			65758
			66789
			66998
			67488
			67511
			68157
			68575
			69713
			69881

```
1 5 9 1 2 2 0 4 7 7 8 7 7 1 2
0 3 3 9 7 2 6 9 7 5 6 1 9 5 5
1 1 5 4 8 9 8 8 3 7 8 9 5 3 8
3 3 3 0 7 7 9 1 5 8 9 1 3 0 8
1 4 5 8 0 3 0 1 9 7 9 5 8 5 4
5 7 2 7 0 1 1 4 1 4 4 2 3 1 7
0 0 5 8 9 5 7 9 3 1 2 4 7 0 6
8 2 3 1 7 9 6 7 3 5 9 5 9 2 8
1 9 3 5 6 9 7 1 8 1 7 1 8 7 2
2 8 1 5 9 8 4 9 5 2 3 5 9 1 3
7 3 7 7 1 8 1 3 2 7 9 7 1 1 5
1 5 5 6 6 9 9 8 7 8 3 8 7 1 7
8 9 1 1 3 1 1 9 3 5 8 5 7 9 5
6 8 3 8 0 8 1 4 4 9 8 9 8 6 8
2 7 4 5 6 4 9 7 6 5 3 1 1 1 6
```

Each term below has a number following it in parentheses, which refers to the numbered dashes below the diagram. Each word forms a box, reading clockwise or counterclockwise. (LAMINATE has already been boxed to start you off.) As you find each term in the diagram, enter the unused letter that's in the middle of each box on the correspondingly numbered dash below the diagram ("N" has already been entered). When you have finished, the letters on the dashes will spell out the title of a popular adventure story.

ALTHOUGH (7)
ANYWHERE (20)
AQUARIUM (1)
BRIGHTEN (16)
CHILDREN (4)
CONSPIRE (22)
DIRECTED (9)
FOOTBALL (14)
GONDOLAS (2)
HIGHBROW (10)
IDENTIFY (8)
~~LAMINATE~~ (19)
LANGUAGE (11)
MACARONI (17)
MYSTICAL (12)
RESEARCH (6)
SEQUENCE (21)
SERENITY (15)
SHIMMERY (5)
TURNOVER (18)
VOLITION (3)
WEDDINGS (13)

```
N A E V O F L S Y M M I T I
Y R E S O Y L E G E V O E L
W E D E T B A M A R I N V O
S L D F C O N G U T U R H G
G N I R E N S O Q A M B R I
D E N E R I P N E V Q U O H
I S T S Y T O D F O O G S T
Y F I I M D B H G W N H A L
B A C A L E R A I L D O L A
I R B M N T O W H S R H C I
G O N I N A E S C N E I R U
H T E R Y S R W T E S E A Q
R I P E W H E E U C O Q E S
U L A M M I D D R N E U Q R
```

__ __ __ __ __ __ __ __ __ __ __ __ __ __ __ __ __ __ N __ __ __
1 2 3   4 5 6 7 8   9 10 11 12 13 14 15 16 17 18 19 20 21 22

If you can SUSTAIN your concentration, you'll have no trouble GATHERing the 44 terms in this Tanglewords.

AFTER	CLUTTERED	FORESIGHT	LAWFUL
APPOINT	CREEL	FORK	LICORICE
ASSIGNMENT	DISCIPLE	GATHER	LOOMED
BIAS	DRAPE	GLIMPSE	MEDITATION
BURNISH	DRAWL	HAIRLINE	METRIC
CAMEO	ENDEAR	INTIMATE	MUSKY
CARGO	FILIBUSTER	ITEM	NUTRITION
			OCTOPUS
			OFFENSE
			PRECEDENT
			PREEMPT
			PROXY
			REDACT
			RESISTANT
			SHELF
			SUBSIDENCE
			SUGGEST
			SUSTAIN
			TONE
			TRANSPOSED
			WADE
			WINCED
			WISECRACK

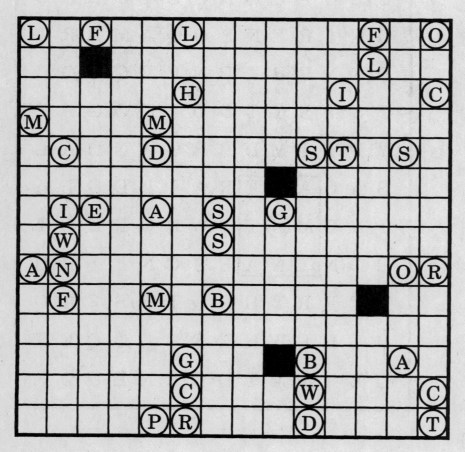

Do battle with this puzzle to locate 36 words containing the letter sequence W-A-R. See how long it takes you to be victorious.

AWARD

AWARE

AWKWARD

BACKWARD

BEWARE

DWARF

EASTWARD

FLATWARE

FORWARD

HARDWARE

HOMEWARD

ONWARD

REWARD

SEAWARD

STEWARD

SWARD

SWARM

THWART

TINWARE

TOWARD

UNWARY

WARBLER

WARDEN

WARDER

WARDROBE

WAREROOM

WARLOCK

WARMTH

WARM-UP

WARN

WARP

WARRANT

WARREN

WARTHOG

WESTWARD

WINDWARD

```
A D R A W T S E W A R D E R
E W A S H E R T I N W A R E
R W E W A R B L E R O A D W
A A A A W A Q U N W A R Y A
W R S R S W A R M L A G P R
T L T D N E D R A W W R E D
A O W O R B A C K W A R D R
L C A I N O M W W W R N R A
F K R A N R A M A A E P A W
R U D W A D T N A R R A W E
A L A F O R W A R D D M O M
W R R D R A W A R M U P T O
D A Z R A W W A R T H O G H
W M O O R E R A W D R A H S
```

The terms in this puzzle are cities in Arkansas. You'll find them hidden diagonally, horizontally or vertically on all three sides of the cube-shaped diagram. One term may be entirely hidden on one face of the cube or it may bend into a second, or a third. HOXIE has been circled as a starter.

ALTUS	DYESS	HAZEN	PARIS
AMITY	EARLE	HOXIE	RISON
BEEBE	EMMET	KIRBY	RONDO
CABOT	FOUKE	LAMAR	SALEM
DESHA	GOULD	LEOLA	VIOLA
DOVER	GRADY	MCRAE	WALDO
DUMAS	HARDY	OZARK	WYNNE

Solve this puzzle like the one on the opposite page, but this time search for Connecticut cities.

BALTIC	DURHAM	MOODUS	SHARON
BANTAM	GILMAN	MOOSUP	SOMERS
BERLIN	GRANBY	MYSTIC	STORRS
BETHEL	GROTON	ORANGE	VERNON
CANAAN	HAMDEN	OXFORD	WESTON
CANTON	MARION	PUTNAM	WILTON
DARIEN			

MATH FUN

Here's another puzzle that tests your math skills. To solve, first determine the answer to the first problem, then take the answer to solve the second problem, and so on, until you have solved all 27. Then look for the answers in the puzzle diagram on the facing page. Your final answer should be THREE.

1. 126 − 67 = _____

2.   + 21 = _____

3.   ÷ 16 = _____

4.   × 18 = _____

5.   − 62 = _____

6.   ÷ 7 = _____

7.   × 17 = _____

8.   + 22 = _____

9.   ÷ 18 = _____

10.   × 12 = _____

11.   ÷ 30 = _____

12.   + 89 = _____

13.   − 58 = _____

14.   × 3 = _____

15.   − 61 = _____

16.   − 35 = _____

17.   × 4 = _____

18.   + 39 = _____

19.   − 44 = _____

20.   + 6 = _____

21.   − 9 = _____

22.   × 20 = _____

23.   ÷ 16 = _____

24.   × 10 = _____

25.   − 33 = _____

26.   + 14 = _____

27.   − 28 = _____

```
O T Y E F T O T S E V E N N
F H V T F I H O H E I N I N
I I M I H I V I T R E N A E
F R F I R G V E R H E Y W E
T T M T H G I E Y T N E W T
Y Y E T Y G A E Y Y Y E E N
O E M A H N I N E T Y O N E
N I V T E R I O S R E O N V
E G Y L U N E N L I U N L E
E H O O E O O E E H X O I S
O T F O O W W W S T C T F N
T H G I E Y T X I S Y E Y E
```

See list of numbers at end of answer section.

The phrase ''lock, stock and barrel'' sounds like it relates to a country store: its front-door lock, its entire stock, and its barrels of inventory. However, it has a totally different origin.

The phrase ''lock, stock and barrel'' means everything or the whole works. The saying refers to the firing mechanism, the rear handle, and the cylindrical chamber of a firearm, or the lock, stock and barrel, which are the essential parts. Thus the phrase literally means ''the whole gun.''

```
S N A E M E S A R H P E H T
B A R R E L H G S A V E B H
N T G S A O K T K E H M A E
A U H R N H L C R T F R R R
H D G E S W O Y O O L A R E
C D A F P E T T W L K E E A
Y N M E C H A N I S M R L R
L A K R I T R G H D E I R D
I K R N C Y N A N S T F G C
N C G G N I Y A S E H T K H
D O L A R A K N R E E M C A
R T P I R C N A E T W I O M
I S F A O E L D N A H O L B
C D E T R L T O T W O U M E
A T S L Y T D H S H L P S R
L A I T N E S S E R E O F A
```

If you consider yourself more of a weekend warrior than a professional sportsperson, you'll appreciate the statement that is hidden in the diagram. To find, it, circle the names of the 25 sporting activities listed below. The leftover letters will reveal the hidden answer.

BADMINTON

BASEBALL

BASKETBALL

BOWLING

CRICKET

CROQUET

FENCING

FOOTBALL

GOLF

HOCKEY

HORSESHOES

JAI ALAI

JOGGING

LACROSSE

NINEPINS

PING-PONG

POLO

SKATING

SNOOKER

SOCCER

SOFTBALL

SQUASH

TENNIS

TRACK AND FIELD

VOLLEYBALL

```
P S E O H S E S R O H R L D
N I N E P I N S A Y S E I L
C N E S S O R C A L K C G E
S R C R O Q U E T P A C O I
Y R I K H T L L A B T O O F
V E E C S S L I S H I S G D
O R K A K A A R D W N O N N
L J R C B E B U K F G O O A
L A O E O R T W Q H I T P K
E I S G C H F H S S N Y G C
Y A O P G B O W L I N G N A
B L U O D I S O M N N O I R
A A F L O G N D T G E N P T
L I T O P A A G N I C N E F
L I L L A B T E K S A B D T
```

DICKENS' ZOO

Charles Dickens is considered one of the major figures in English literature. In addition to portraying men, women, and children with the sharp insight of a great storyteller, he presented various animals in his stories that were quite memorable. We've hidden the names of 31 of these animals in the diagram below. Can you find them all?

BOXER	DICK	HOPE
CARLO	DIOGENES	JIP
CAULIFLOWER	DUST	JOY
CUNNING	EDDARD	JUNO
DAPH	GRIP	LIFE
		LION
		LOVELY
		MERRYLEGS
		PEACE
		PEDRO
		PINCHER
		PLUNDER
		PONTO
		RAGS
		REST
		RUIN
		SPINACH
		WHISKER
		WIGS
		WORDS
		YOUTH

```
Y R R E K S I H W P E R
O C E L D C U N N I N G
J A H C A N I P S R G I
Y U C T S U D D E G N S
J L N W R A R S N F O G
R I I O H O R D E P I E
O F P T W P B C G L L L
P L U V S G A R O U O Y
X O R E B E Z D I N V R
Y W N A P D R A D D E R
G E S T C O R Q U E L E
E R E X O B H C H R Y M
```

Listed below are 36 six-letter words, each of which has three syllables. Can you find them all hidden in the diagram?

AERIAL
ALUMNA
ANIMAL
ANNUAL
AVENUE
BANANA
CALICO
CAMERA
CANARY
CAVIAR
CELERY
DYNAMO
EDITOR
ELEVEN
ERASER
GALAXY
ICICLE
INDIGO
IRONIC
LIVERY
MARACA
MEDIAN
MEDIUM
MELODY
NOTIFY
ORIGIN

PERIOD
PODIUM
POETRY
POTATO
RADIUS

REMEDY
TUXEDO
UNEASY
UNEVEN
ZODIAC

```
O I C E L N A M C A V I A R
Z G A L A X Y N N I Z F Y N
N O I I M C S M Q O N R X E
R I D D I A U Y R T E O P L
E E G I N L I D A V A B R C
M V B I A I D O I R E P E I
E N A U R C A L O Z A L Y C
D Y N A M O R E X T E B X I
Y N A E P A D M A R A C A R
A R N E V E L E Y F I T O N
E D A E S E R D X S J T O A
M I N N G I N I M U I D O P
Y U N E A S Y U S D T Y L Z
E M E L O C A M E R A S E R
```

When you look for the terms in this puzzle, you'll find that each bends at an angle. DUCHESS is outlined to show you how. There are 30 other titles hidden below, and none of the terms overlap. Can you find them all?

BARON

BARONESS

CHIEF

COUNT

CZAR

CZARINA

DAUPHIN

DOGE

DUCHESS

DUKE

EARL

EMPEROR

EMPRESS

KHAN

KING

KNIGHT

LADY

LORD

MAJESTY

MIKADO

NOBLEMAN

PHARAOH

PRINCE

PRINCESS

QUEEN

RAJAH

ROYALTY

RULER

SOVEREIGN

SULTAN

VISCOUNT

```
A L T Y H P U A D O Y T S E
E Y R O R I R A Z J A R J O
R P O E U A N K C A A A U C
O K M R L G N I L H M N G S
R I N E H A N T D U T E O I
T H G I K Z A U O C S A D V
R E V O S N C N C R N A M E
E H S S E H E P E Z A N E L
I S O R Y S H L R A A B E B
G S A A S A D P A N I R U O
N E D L R R R S S E R E Q N
O C Y L O I N C E Y B P K D
D N I R P T H E I H C A M U
A K I M N U O C F U N O R E
```

HOMOPHONE HALVES —————————————————

Homophones are words that sound the same but have different spellings and meanings, such as ADDS and ADZE. To solve this puzzle, write the homophone for each word below; then find both words in the diagram, for a total of 38 words.

<u>ADDS</u> ADZE

_____ BANNED

_____ BREACH

_____ QUIRE

_____ SHOOT

_____ DEER

_____ ENTRANTS

_____ FLOWER

_____ GRISLY

_____ HARE

_____ LIEF

_____ MASSED

_____ FRAYS

_____ SLOE

_____ STAKE

_____ SON

_____ SERGE

_____ TRACKED

_____ WAIST

```
T W S Y N C D E K C A R T G
S S N E O L N R A E D M A R
E T U T S T T I S D D L E I
B E N S R E C T E H S W O Z
H A L A B A A E R U O L F Z
C K N W R K R I D L H O W L
E C E D E T T M F E I L T Y
E A W B A N N E D O S A L E
R O C I C W M E R U Y S C H
B E L H H E T S N W I U A E
I R O S U S G A Y R T R W M
R I A H I T D R G A E G O A
R U L A G Z E H E L R E L S
D Q W L E A F P H S M F S T
```

See word list at end of answer section.

GISELLE is ballet's great tragedy and *COPPÉLIA* is its great comedy. Both ballets are love stories and are performed regularly by ballet companies. Trip the light fantastic and search for these and 32 other ballets hidden in the puzzle below.

ABYSS
AGON
ANASTASIA
APOLLO

ARENA
ASTARTE
AUREOLE
BALLADE

BHAKTI
BIOSFERA
BLUEBEARD
BUGAKU
CAGE (The)
CARD GAME
CARMEN
CHACONNE
CIRCLES
COPPÉLIA
DON JUAN
DUEL (The)
FANFARE
FOUR SEASONS
GEMINI
GISELLE
GUESTS (The)
HAMLET
HI-KYO
INCUBUS
JEWELS
JINX
JIVE
JOB
MANON
MEDEA

```
P S C W A S T A R T E E V O
G L A B N U T N A U J N O D
F E R R L B A S N Z A N C Y
A W M F O U R S E A S O N S
N E E I R C E W R U P C O B
F J N E N N F B A P G A N A
A M O Z L I S P E J N H A E
R L E E S T O L Q A I C M M
E G U L E L I U S K R N E A
E D A L L A B T Y I H D X G
B V M O C E A O K A E E U D
A A I M R S S Y B A G W J R
H A M J I D E I N C H O K A
C E G A C U K A G U B B N C
```

The NUTCRACKER has become an annual Christmas tradition in many American and Canadian cities. In fact, in New York City, it has been performed every Christmas since 1954! See if you can find NUTCRACKER and 30 other ballets hidden below.

NAPOLI

NOCES (Les)

NUTCRACKER (The)

OCTUOR

ODE

OLYMPICS

ONDINE

ORPHEUS

PAGANINI

PAQUITA

PAVANE

PERI (La)

RAYMONDA

REVERIES

RITUALS

RIVER (The)

RODEO

ROOMS

SEBASTIAN

SONATINE

SWAN LAKE

SYLVIA

TARANTELLA

TILT

TRACES

TRIAD

TZADDIK

TZIGANE

VALSE (La)

VESTRIS

WHO CARES?

```
L S I A N S S E R A C O H W
Y C Y L T G E M N O C E S N
S A R L O N D I N E U I U N
N W I E V A N H R M G T O A
X T A T Z I G A N E C Y C P
O P Q N N T A P L R V G S O
L I V A L S E C A R T E I L
Y L G R B A Y C H R R E R I
M A I A Z B K I D D A Z T S
P E L T R E O E A T Y D S U
I A C I R S D Z I R M F E E
C M V O H T E U R Y O W V H
S E O A S S Q K T L N D O P
R M S O N A T I N E D J E R
S E V N P E R I T U A L S O
```

Hold onto your hats while you search for 23 types of winds and windstorms hidden below.

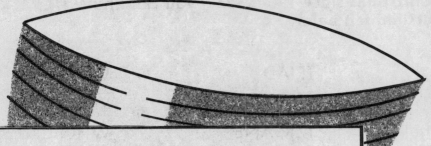

```
I L B I H G E S H A M A L
C K Z O N A I S E T E S A
W H E M R V B H A T I O R
N A M N K A N O E R L D T
A M C N O O S N O M T A S
T S M N O L A C I B E N I
T I U Q N C C H N S E R M
A N Q K I O T Y P H O O N
M G N R H S Q R C A O T A
R Q R L C O U E L R M F R
A U T E J K V E D A R T U
H S W Y B E A E E V E J B
L S E I L L I W Y L L I W
```

BERG

BORA

BURAN

CHINOOK

CYCLONE

ETESIAN

FÖHN

GHIBLI

HABOOB

HARMATTAN

HURRICANE

KHAMSIN

LEVECHE

MISTRAL

MONSOON

SHAMAL

SHARAV

SIROCCO

SUKHOVEY

TORNADO

TRADE

TYPHOON

WILLY WILLIES

ANTELOPEs and DEER belong in the category of hoofed ruminants. However, there are differences between the two species. The antlers of DEER are branched and are shed, whereas the ANTELOPE's antlers are not branched and are not shed. Can you find all 32 varieties hidden below?

ADDAX

ANTELOPE

AXIS

BLESBOK

BONGO

BROCKET

CARIBOU

CHAMOIS

DEER

DIK-DIK

DUIKER

ELAND

ELK

GAZELLE

GEMSBOK

GERENUK

GNU

IMPALA

KUDU

MHOR

MOOSE

MUNTJAC

NILGHAI

NYALA

ORYX

REINDEER

SABLE

SAIGA

SAMBAR

SITATUNGA

SPRINGBOK

WAPITI

```
K I B R D O M U N T J A C E
G O Y D U I K E R O B E L K
D X B R O C K E T J G L T G
N I L G H A I D S A E N S N
A K E A N R W A I Z P I O U
L U S M Y I M Z A K O R Y B
E D B L O B R G E M S B O K
I U O C A O N P A C O R A U
S M K R K U S H S K Y J L N
W A P I T I C E A X I S A E
B O K A M H O R B D A C Y R
A N T E L O P E L M E D N E
J I A G I A S T E W O E D G
S M R E E D N I E R B I R A
```

Among the many scientists and inventors who have been honored on US postage stamps are Elias HOWE, who built and patented the first sewing machine, and physicist Albert EINSTEIN. Hidden below are HOWE, EINSTEIN, and the names of 22 other honored Americans.

AUDUBON (John J.)

BAILEY (Liberty Hyde)

BELL (Alexander G.)

BURBANK (Luther)

CARVER (George W.)

COPERNICUS (Nicolaus)

EASTMAN (George)

EDISON (Thomas A.)

EINSTEIN (Albert)

FRANKLIN (Benjamin)

FULTON (Robert)

GODDARD (Robert)

HOWE (Elias)

LONG (Dr. Crawford)

MAYO (Drs. William and Charles)

MCCORMICK (Cyrus)

MCDOWELL (Dr. Ephraim)

MORSE (Samuel F.B.)

PAPANICOLAOU (Dr. George)

REED (Dr. Walter)

WHITNEY (Eli)

WRIGHT (Orville, Wilbur)

```
P Q L D M C D O W E L L
B A I L E Y J H A A V M
C O P E R N I C U S O C
A N T A Q T E N D T W C
R I M E N X E Z U M R O
V L A E I I N W B A I R
E K Y W E O C L O N G M
R N O P T E M O N H H I
A A L L S B E L L O T C
D R U R N B U R B A N K
A F O T I D R A D D O G
I M R E E D I S O N C U
```

The first modern postage stamp, the "penny black," was issued in England on May 1, 1840. Solve this puzzle and learn an amusing postage stamp story.

The world
licking
record
was set
in London
in July,
nineteen
sixty-
five,
when a
twenty-
four-
hour
lick-in
resulted
in the
sticking
of almost
three
hundred
thousand
postage
stamps.
There
is no

report
as to
whether
all those

envelopes
were
ever
mailed.

```
G N I K C I L B L Y O R F S
O N O U G H D N A S U O H T
I X I R E S U L T E D T L A
S N I K C I L F R Z R S M M
V E J C C Z J M I O T A I P
N U P U A I A E P V W V N S
O C H O L I T E G L E E T H
D S Y J L Y R S F A N E H W
N I N E T E E N O G T Z E T
O X D R H V V T U M Y S O Z
L T R T O O H N R W L N O V
N Y E C S R U T E S S A W P
I H V R E C O R D I X N F F
W J E E L D E R D N U H P O
```

BIOGRAPHY: LOUIS BRAILLE

Having lost his eyesight at an early age, Louis Braille overcame his handicap and eventually perfected a system of reading and writing that has helped a countless number of people afflicted with blindness lead normal lives. You can read more about Braille below. Words grouped together in the word list will be found together in the diagram on the opposite page.

Louis
Braille,
a Frenchman who
became blind
at the
age of
three,
was the
inventor
of a special
system of
reading
and writing
for the
blind.
The Braille
system
involves
patterns
of raised
dots
which
are read

by touching
them.
Writing is
done
by punching
tiny
holes
in paper
stretched
across
a frame.
Louis Braille
was also
a fine
musician,
well
known
all over
France
for his
organ
playing.

```
E M A R F A J T H E B R A I L L E L
S E V L O V N I W R I T I N G I S D
C T M U S I C I A N R E V O L L A B
J S Z Q C E Q I P N D Q H O Q E H Y
C Y T F E Z L A Z D D O H T R Q C P
D S C R Q L P L E C C W N E S Z I U
N C H A E E J S I N N Q R E Q A H N
I T Q N R T I M S A J A V I G J W C
L Z U C Q A C E M G R Q Z E T P C H
B A Q E R Z L H F R R B O F A I G I
E N I F A O C T E O Z F S T S A N N
M F O C H N Z S T D M Q T I Q C I G
A C O W E L L N I Q Z E H V U R Y N
C C Q R Z P E V S U R R T Q C O A I
E Y F C T V S T K N O W N S Z S L D
B A N V N H O A S F Q L Z J Y S P A
Z B L I N D E Z F C W A S A L S O E
C E H T T A B Y T O U C H I N G Q R
```

PRODUCING PRODUCE ――――――――――――――――――

Fill in the dashes below with a fruit or vegetable to make a phrase or title. Then find the filled-in word in the puzzle diagram. As a help, the answers are in alphabetical order.

1. *The* ―――――― *Dumpling Gang*

2. "*The* ―――――― *Boat Song*"

3. Orson ――――――

4. Red as a ――――――

5. "―――――― Hill"

6. ―――――― Patch Kid

7. Dangle a ――――――

8. ―――――― ear

9. ――――――stone clam

10. ―――――― Grove

11. *The* ―――――― *Is Green*

12. Cool as a ――――――

13. Heard on the ――――――vine

14. ―――――― *Finn*

15. *The* ―――――― *Drop Kid*

16. "――――――house Blues"

17. *The* ―――――― *Tree*

18. *The* ―――――― *Field*

19. *A Clockwork* ――――――

20. Georgia ――――――

21. ――――――-shaped diamond

22. Like two ―――――― in a pod

23. *The Great Waldo* ――――――

24. "―――――― Princess"

25. Sugar―――――― fairy

26. Mr. ―――――― Head

27. Wrinkled as a ――――――

28. *A* ―――――― *in the Sun*

29. Darryl ――――――

30. *Fried Green* ――――――

31. ―――――― *Man*

```
C V W R E W O L F I L U A C
T O R R A C C N B O G N A M
R X C Y Z O J A I K Q B D B
Y E F O R A N G E O B G R H
R K P N A A P L R A N A E Y
R Y M P N N C P G A I N L R
E R P A E R U E L S P H P R
B R R T S P C T I E C E P E
E E U P E P U N T A V E A B
L B N O L E M R E T A W E W
K E E U W X B P M S Y A N A
C U M N O M E L I Z N J I R
U L C H E R R Y L R A E P T
H B P O T A T O M A T O E S
```

See word list at end of answer section.

"F" FRENZY

Whether you're a FARMER, a FEMALE, a member of a college FACULTY or even a FLY, everyone's FREE to solve this puzzle filled with words that begin with the letter "F." We think it's more enjoyable than a hot FUDGE ice cream sundae!

FACIAL	FEUD	FOAM
FACULTY	FEW	FOE
FAIL	FIERCE	FOIL
FAIR	FIFE	FOMENT
FAKE	FIG	FOOL
FALL	FILE	FOR
FAME	FILL	FORCE
FANCY	FIN	FORD
FAR	FIR	FOUR
FARE	FIREFLY	FRACTION
FARMER	FISH	FRAGMENT
FARO	FIVE	FRAME
FATAL	FIX	FRANKLY
FATE	FLAKE	FREE
FAVORITE	FLAME	FRO
FEAR	FLAW	FROLIC
FED	FLAX	FRUIT
FEE	FLEW	FUDGE
FEEL	FLIGHT	FUEL
FELL	FLIMSY	FUNGUS
FELLOW	FLUX	FUNNY
FEMALE	FLY	FURNACE
FEND	FOAL	FURY

```
F I F E F T E C A N R U F D
A D I F I R E F L Y I R R U
T N E M G A R F I X A O A E
A E R Y R U F E I C F F N F
L F C F I R T L T S F A K E
Y A E T O I U I I U H C L L
S I F L R A O O D G T U Y L
M L I O F N M G F N H L O I
I C V L O L E R E U E T A F
L A E S E L A M E F N Y I S
F W A L F M O M O M C N E R
W O L L E F A R E N R L Y A
E K A L F U C F A C I A L E
F X U L F E F F T F E D F F
```

Introduced in 1891, basketball is now played around the world in more than 100 countries. We're sure that you won't need an ASSIST to find these 30 words associated with basketball.

ASSIST	CORNER MAN	DUNK
BASKET	COURT	FIELD GOAL
BUCKET	DEFENSE	FORWARD
CENTER	DRIBBLE	FOUL
		FOUL LINE
		FREE THROW
		GUARD
		JUMPER
		LAYUP
		PENALTY
		PIVOT
		PLAY
		POINTS
		PRESS
		REBOUND
		SCORE
		SET SHOT
		SHOOT
		STEAL
		THREE-POINT PLAY
		TRAVELING
		VIOLATION

```
Y T P N B Z H P E N A L T Y
K W R Z A T T E K C U B A Q
N U E A S M D S T E A L V K
U B S I V N R R Y N P J I T
D A S A U E Z E S T N I O P
R S F O U L L I N E K O L J
A K B Q A B Z I R R H A A O
W E R Y B Q O T N S O Z T S
R T U I G P R Q O G B C I C
O P R J E U J E D H L Q O O
F D S E Z Y A L P J S U N R
W O R H T E E R F M R T O E
R H T O V I P R D T U Y E F
T E D E F E N S E Y D J L S
```

Bill **BRADLEY** attended Princeton University and earned a Rhodes scholarship at Oxford University after graduation. He then signed on with the New York Knicks and is now a US senator. Look for BRADLEY and the names of 34 other pro cagers who are honored in the Basketball Hall of Fame.

ARCHIBALD (Nate)
BARRY (Rick)
BAYLOR (Elgin)
BING (Dave)
BRADLEY (Bill)
CERVI (Al)
CHAMBERLAIN (Wilt)
COUSY (Bob)
COWENS (Dave)
FRAZIER (Walt)
FULKS (Joe)
GALE (Lauren)
GATES (William)
GOLA (Tom)
GREER (Hal)
HAGAN (Cliff)
HAVLICEK (John)
HAYES (Elvin)
JONES (K.C.; Sam)
LUCAS (Jerry)
MARAVICH (Pete)
MARTIN (Slater)
MIKAN (George)
MONROE (Earl)
PAGE (Pat)
PETTIT (Bob)
RAMSEY (Frank)

REED (Willis)
ROBERTSON (Oscar)
RUSSELL (Bill)
SCHAYES (Adolph)

SHARMAN (Bill)
UNSELD (Wes)
WEST (Jerry)
WILKENS (Lenny)

```
H C I V A R A M A N A G A H
Y R R A B N N A M R A H S A
D N B O N I B U G L E R E V
L O A F A T N Q E O P B Y L
A S Y K K R U G P R L R A I
B T L N I A L R E B M A H C
I R O N Y M E E T P A D R E
H E R O S S D E T R O L E K
C B L I U E L R I U T E I X
R O B V O Y E C T S K Y Z S
A R W R C A S P T S E W A E
J O N E S H N A M E S C R T
I O N C N C U G A L U F F A
M F U L K S N E K L I W A G
```

To solve this puzzle, insert a letter from below into each of the circles in the diagram. This letter should be one that will let you form as many 5-letter words as possible. If you have entered the correct letters into the circles, you should be able to find 49 words in total. We've inserted the letter "L" to start you off.

C	D	H	J	L̸	M	N	P	R	S	T

YOUR WORD LIST

```
M S V O C G S B N A H R D W
C H S H A L E G A L A B E H
E A I V Y O A M E O A L L Y
E O A L F V H S I E G O O S
P E Y Z Y E A O H R A E O S
L T L H Y O N A C I J O A S
M O Y T T E O O K E R E T Z
Y T O I M A E N S T A O E Y
E U I E R W R S E O E I D R
R L V Y R T K E C W O U E R
O N T G N I Y O L I U Q R A
U A C E H M E U A C U B I O
O H O R N T I D S I L Q U E
E J L I L R A E O A I N T D
```

See word list at end of answer section.

Below are the scrambled names of 26 items found in a tool shed. After you unscramble the names, you will have an alphabetized list of the words hidden in the diagram. We've unscrambled OLSTB into BOLTS, and circled it in the diagram to start you off.

1. OLSTB __BOLTS__

2. KETCBU _____

3. ELSHIC _____

4. LILRD _____

5. EIFL _____

6. MEMARH _____

7. SOHE _____

8. DEDALR _____

9. AHLTE _____

10. WNLA OERWM _____

11. VEELL _____

12. LAISN _____

13. ERPILS _____

14. KARE _____

15. DASNRPEAP _____

16. DREWSCIRVER _____

17. VELHSO _____

18. OCKTES TSE _____

19. APSTLER _____

20. BLTAE WSA _____

21. LOTO ESCHT _____

22. SEVI _____

23. ELEHWRABWOR _____

24. RWEI _____

25. CHENBKRWO _____

26. CHERNW _____

```
W O R R A B L E E H W C Q J
C O A V E H T A L T O R Z E
R K R Z Q H J E A Q E S R Q
E J V K J C Z B K W J I E W
V L Z Y B N L Q O C W Q M S
I A S C Q E J M Q Z U T M A
R D J T S R N A I L S B A N
D D J A A W C C Z E C D H D
W E W Q A P Z L H Q R C J P
E R S L C V L C E I J Z L A
R F Q I Z Q L E L V S I Q P
C Z I J V O J L R J E E J E
S (S T L O B) V Q Z R C L L R
T E S T E K C O S H O V E L
```

See word list at end of answer section.

PHRASE PLAY ————————————————————————————————

Welcome to "Phrase Play." Each column below represents a portion of a cliché or a familiar phrase. Column A is the beginning, Column B is the middle, and Column C is the end. Select an entry from each column and put them together to form a common phrase. After you have connected all the phrases, you can then find each column entry in the diagram.

A	B	C
BE IN THE	A SPADE	A FALL
CALL	A SWEET	AFTER BAD
CARRY	A TORCH	A SPADE
EASY	BETWEEN	CABOODLE
GET A	COME	EASY GO
GIVE A	DRIVER'S	FANTASTIC
HAVE	ENDS AGAINST	FOR
HEADING	FOR	PRESENT
LIKE A FISH	GOOD MONEY	SEAT
NO TIME	HEADS	STRIDE
PLAY BOTH	IT IN	THE ACTION
PUT YOUR	KIT AND	THE BRIDGE
READ	LIKE THE	THE LINES
SEE WHICH	OUT OF	THE MIDDLE
TAKE	PIECE OF	TOGETHER
THE WHOLE	PIECE OF	TOOTH
THROW	THE LIGHT	WATER
TRIP	UNDER	WIND BLOWS
WATER	WAY THE	YOUR MIND

```
I P E N O I T C A E H T S D F I T
L D R I V E R S P T L E A A O H C
I T A E M I T O N R N E N L E E A
K O T A S P A D E I R T K L C A B
E G E H T E K I L P A E I A E D O
A E G F R T N E I S T G T F I I O
F T R O A O H T T S H Y A A P N D
I H F K A T W I E T E S N S W G L
S E E W H I C H R N W A D P D R E
H R T E E W S A G U H E T A S N L
D A E V I G W O N Y O U N D E R E
N W H G C P O D E E L Y A E A C L
I P A N O D L E H R E E T F M A D
M I V T M S B A T T H W T U T R D
R E E O E T D S Y E O E T O P R I
U C N U L R N Y A B R O R E O Y M
O E I T L I I G W B O C T F B I E
Y O T O A D W O A E H T N I E B H
O F I F C E G D I R B E H T B E T
```

See phrases at end of answer section.

With the success of television's "Batman," big celebrities were eager to accept small cameo roles so they could be seen on this "happening" show. Here are some of the entertainers who appeared either as themselves or as a character they were known to portray. We've circled HALE to start you off.

BARRY (Jack)
BERLE (Milton)
BESSER (Joe)
BROLIN (James)

CASSIDY (Ted)
CLARK (Dick)
CORBY (Ellen)
DANA (Bill)

DAVIS (Sammy, Jr.)
DILLER (Phyllis)
DON HO
DOZIER (William)
DUFF (Howard)
FERRARE (Cindy)
GARR (Teri)
HALE (Alan, Jr.)
HORWITZ (Howie)
JAFFE (Sam)
KLEMPERER (Werner)
KNICKERBOCKER (Susie)
LEE (Bruce, Gypsy Rose)
LEWIS (Jerry)
LINKLETTER (Art)
LORIMER (Louise)
MATHERS (Jerry)
OWENS (Gary)
RAFT (George)
REEVES (Dick)
REINER (Rob)
ROBINSON (Edward G.)
SCHINE (G. David)
STANG (Arnold)
STRANGIS (Judy)
WILLIAMS (Van)
YOUNGMAN (Henny)

```
N Y S C H I N E G O W E N S
I J R M I J E R N G R N I Y
F E R R A R E S A E A M L C
K H E D A I K Z T I W R O H
Q N M J N B L T S U T H R E
M P I E Z R E L L I D F B S
O S R C H L M S I V A D A T
X I O A K B P I Z W A Y N R
L W L N R E E V E S D R W A
E E I A A Q R O B I N S O N
L L E M L Y E B S E R X E G
Y F Z G C X R S O E S F L I
K B F N A N A D H C F S R S
H A R U N C M T A A K Z E G
O H N O D E A L J A K E B R
J T H Y C M D D O Z I E R B
```

If you're looking for BAT CAVE, you don't have to go to Gotham City: try North Carolina instead. You can also find the capitals of Michigan, Delaware, and Colorado there. This puzzle contains the names of 42 small towns in the TAR HEEL State.

ACME
ALMA
AVON
BAT CAVE
BATH
BOOMER
CARY
CASAR
DANA
DEEP GAP
DENVER
DOVER
EARL
EDEN
ENON
FAITH
GATES
GULF
IVANHOE
KITTY HAWK
KONA
LANSING
LENOIR
LORAY
MAGNOLIA
MANTEO
MAPLE

MICRO
NAGS HEAD
OCRACOKE
OLIN
OTTO

RED OAK
SHELBY
STAR
TAPOCO
TAR HEEL

TOAST
TURKEY
WATHA
WAVES
WISE

```
R W S D A E H S G A N B K R
C A L H R J Y T Z F N O I C
T R T D E E P G A P L O V M
K A L S K L L Q A B N U K A
W B P R X B N S E T A G G
A A U O A E A Y L W C L N N
H T L E C D E T O A S T I O
Y C F B O O M E R V D L S L
T A Q A H A N Y C E O L N I
T V R N I K M R I S V R A A
I E A O E T N A M I E N L N
K V T N L J H S P W R M E R
I T L E E H R A T L A D C D
O R V O C R A C O K E L W A
```

A ROSE IS A ROSE

Roses have been cultivated throughout the world for many centuries. There are 46 varieties listed with the dates they were first introduced to rose fanciers. The oldest rose, AUTUMN DAMASK, dates from 1200 and is still cultivated today!

ABALARD (1845)

AGAR (1843)

AGNES (1922)

ALBERIC BARBIER (1900)

ARMIDE (1817)

ARNOLD (1893)

AURORA (1956)

AUTUMN DAMASK (1200)

BLANCHEFLEUR (1835)

BLUSH DAMASK (1789)

EMPRESS JOSEPHINE (1853)

GEORGE WILL (1909)

HANSA (1905)

JEANNE D'ARC (1818)

JUNO (1833)

KAZANLIK (1850)

LANEII (1854)

LA NOBLESSE (1835)

LEDA (1827)

MAIDEN'S BLUSH (15th Century)

MARBREE (1888)

MARIE ROBERT (1850)

MAY QUEEN (1898)

MME. BOLL (1859)

MME. DORE (1863)

MME. HARDY (1832)

MME. KNORR (1855)

OEILLET FLAMAND (1845)

OLD BLACK (1845)

PROSERPINE (1841)

QUEEN OF BEDDARS (1871)

RAPHEL (1856)

REVELL (1852)

ROBERT LE DIABLE (1850)

ROSA BLANDA (1773)

ROSE DU ROI (1815)

SALET (1854)

SANDER'S WHITE (1910)

SPONG (1805)

SWAMP ROSE (1726)

TORCH (1942)

TUSCANY (1596)

UNIQUE BLANCHE (1775)

VIVID (1853)

WHITE BATH (1810)

WILLIAM LOBB (1855)

```
T M A I D E N S B L U S H D A M A S K R
U A A U N T J E A N N E D A R C W A S U
B Y E R T U S C A N Y A S E M A Z L A E
B Q G R I U A R O R U A I E M A S E N L
O U S P O E M A R N A B S P N N E T D F
L E P O H S R N R O R D R L A G K N E E
M E I L K M A O D A N O I I E N A L R H
A N L L I M H B B A S K L P P I L S S C
I O L D L A M C L E M M E B O L L P W N
L F E O N E I E D A R A I M A T R O H A
L B D S O R T U H B N T S Y M O P N I L
I E A L E L R F R A E D L K S R L G T B
W D A B O O D A L A R A A E H C E G E E
E D L S I N C B M A C D R R D H H N B U
G A T L T T R A L X M P Y S T I P I A Q
R R G F Z O R A R A I A N U T N A R T I
O S A A A B B J R N C I N C H A R B H N
E R Q D R A U G E R T K T D I V I V L U
G A S E E N I H P E S O J S S E R P M E
M M E D O R E V E L L A N O B L E S S E
```

Japanese Kabuki drama integrates movement, music and language so that no single element dominates. It is also notable for its use of only male actors, even for female roles. Search below for 30 traditional Kabuki roles.

AKAHIME (red princess)

AKUBA (wicked woman)

AKU-OJI (wicked priest)

BOZU (Buddhist priest)

BUSHI (warrior)

CHONIN (merchants)

GUMPYO (troops)

HIME (princess)

INAKA NYOBO (country wife)

JOCHU (maid)

KAGOYA (bearers)

KAMURO (attendant)

KINDACHI (young nobles)

KOSHIMOTO (wealthy daughter)

KOSHO (page boy)

KO-YAKU (child)

KUGE (court nobles)

KUGE-AKU (wicked noble)

MACHI NYOBO (city wife)

MEKAKE (mistress)

MIDAIDOKORO (wife of a lord)

MUSUME (girl)

OTOKOGATA (male role)

TAYU (courtesan)

TOBI (fireman)

WAKASHU (a youth)

YABO (naive character)

YAKKO (servant to Samurai)

YAKUZA (idler, gambler)

YUJO (courtesan)

```
J Y A K U Z A G O T M D B A
O I G Z F E U E H U O A C O
N K O T O M I H S O K B R K
O B O A P I H U O P Q U I I
T B R Y M H M N K O M K R N
O L O U P E U H S A K A W D
K M K Y Q R K M K L Y G K A
O B O Y N A K A N I N O H C
G U D T S I H O K K A Y K H
A V I Y X I H Y F E I A J I
T X A H M E Z C A H W Y T S
A B D E S G U K A E G U K U
O B I J O U K A Y M X J V B
E C M D A K B Z U H C O J C
```

Each role in Japanese Kabuki theater has its own traditional and distinctive costume and makeup. Even small accessories such as the TENUGUI and AKOME OGI are extremely important for giving great meaning to simple gestures.

AKOME OGI (folding fan)
AMI-GASA (large hat)
BOKUTO (wooden sword)
BOSHI (head decoration)
BUNKO (obi bow)
DAITO (long sword)
DOGI (undergarment)
EBOSHI (paper hat)
FUNGOMI (women's trousers)
FUSA (tassel)
GETA (wooden clogs)
GOMA (gray wig)
HAKAMA (culottes)
HAKIMONO (footwear)
HANTEN (outer coat)
HAORI (short coat)
HIMO (strings, ties)
HIRAUCHI (hairpin)
HITOE (unlined kimono)
ICHO (hair top knot)
ISHO (costume)

KABUTO (helmet)
KAPPA (raincoat)
KASA (hat)
KATANA (sword)
KATSURA (wig)
KESA (priest's robe)
KESHO (makeup)
KYAHAN (leggings)
MAEDARE (apron)

SAIHAI (baton)
SANE (armor platelets)
TABI (bifurcated socks)
TEKKO (mittens)
TENUGUI (hand towel)
WARAJI (straw sandals)
YUGAKE (gauntlet)
ZORI (thong sandals)
ZUKIN (hood)

```
Z Y A I H S O B B C A D O E F
G U H A H H I I E I J M K L M
N G K H C A A B R O I Z O R I
H A K I M O N O A H T T E G X
K K O A N O A T D T U I C W D
P E K S K H T N E B O S H I I
Q A S K K Y A H A N M O I P J
H O E H B Z K K M L U A H Q A
R T S U O A O K I J P G C R R
F U N G O M I X G P R F U S A
D K T B E K E S A K Z S A I W
O O U O N T C K S G T S R B Y
V B G Y A D A E A A D A I T O
W I X I S H O E K V U T H Z A
```

IT'S A KNOCKOUT! ——————————— 95

Boxing's popularity peaked during the 1920s and 1930s, but it still captures a very large share of fans. Keep your GUARD up and HOOK the 38 boxing terms below.

BELL
BLOCK
BLOWS
BOUT
BREAK

CANVAS
CLINCH
CORNER
CROSS
DECISION

DEFENSE
DUCK
FIST
FOUL
GLOVES
GUARD
HOOK
JAB
JUDGES
KNOCKOUT
MOUTHPIECE
NEUTRAL
(corner)
OFFENSE
PARRY
POINT
POSITION
PULL
PUNCH
REFEREE
REST
RING
ROPES
ROUND
SLIP
STANCE
STRAIGHT
STYLE
TECHNICAL
(knockout)

```
N C R O S S E K N Y P U L L
R O P E S L N E U T R A L U
T R I P Y N K L C G M R T O
U N H T O O F F E N S E A F
O E S C I I T J K I A M N P
B R E T N S N N C R P T E G
A R S E I I O T O A U S S B
J E E F R C L P L C N E T L
R G G A K E D C B E C V R O
Q O D O K D F U F H H O A W
M O U T H P I E C E O L I S
J T J N I L D R R K O G G P
B E L L D R A U G H K L H M
M B S N L A C I N H C E T L
```

112

In professional boxing, the heavyweight class draws the most interest and commands the largest purses. Here are the names of 32 fighters who have all won heavyweight titles.

ALI (Muhammad)

BAER (Max)

BOWE (Riddick)

BRADDOCK (James J.)

BURNS (Tommy)

CARNERA (Primo)

CHARLES (Ezzard)

CORBETT (James J.)

DEMPSEY (Jack)

DOKES (Michael)

ELLIS (Jimmy)

FOREMAN (George)

FRAZIER (Joe)

HART (Marvin)

HOLMES (Larry)

HOLYFIELD (Evander)

LISTON (Sonny)

LOUIS (Joe)

MARCIANO (Rocky)

NORTON (Ken)

PAGE (Greg)

PATTERSON (Floyd)

SCHMELING (Max)

SPINKS (Leon, Michael)

SULLIVAN (John L.)

TATE (John)

TERRELL (Ernie)

TUBBS (Tony)

TUNNEY (Gene)

TYSON (Mike)

WALCOTT (Joe)

WILLARD (Jess)

```
W L E G N I L E M H C S A C
S A L T Y E L N R U T A S H
K I L O K T E T O U Q B O A
N D I C H A R T N S O L S R
I N S H O T R N S W Y M E L
P O Y S L T E P E F I T K E
S T O I M Y T E I T A L O S
U S N U E A Y E S P M E D D
L I A O S O L S B B U T T R
L L I L R D O C A R N E R A
I N C P A T T E R S O N E L
V B R A D D O C K D E C A L
A N A G A E R N S N R U B I
N A M E R O F R A Z I E R W
```

There are a total of 60 terms in this puzzle, and they all have four or more letters. Words entirely within other words are not included. When you finish the puzzle, every letter will have been circled at least once.

ACQUIRE	CLEAN	ERNE	HUGS	LINER
ALIGN	CLOUD	EXCITES	IBIS	LINT
ANEW	CODE	GENT	IDOL	LIST
ANTONYM	COGS	GILL	IRED	MARKS
ARCH	DIAL	GLADIATOR	LASTING	MEND
ARRIVAL	DIGITAL	GLIMMER	LEANT	MERCHANT
BASHFUL	DOCTOR	GONE	LEVITY	MOAN
BEQUEST	DRUG	HIRE	LIBRARIANS	MUSIC
				NASTY
				NITER
				RANG
				RIVET
				SEAR
				SECOND
				SEVERAL
				SHEEN
				SILO
				SQUAD
				STEEL
				STROLLER
				STYLING
				TESTIFY
				TIARA
				TIER
				TIMID
				TORN
				TORRID
				WRIT

```
D I G I T A L I G N E E H S
I S Y F I T S E T I C X E Q
R N B A S H F U L M L C N U
R A M E R C H A N T O L O A
O I A C Q U I R E N U A G D
T R R I G U R D D A D R N L
A A K S T E E L O E I E A E
I R S U M N N S C L M V R V
D B A M W R I T T C I E C I
A I I I R E L L O R T S H T
L L A S T I N G R I V E T Y
G N I L Y T S A N T O N Y M
```

114

This is a Word Search in reverse. Circled letters are the initial letters of one or more words, and any letter may be part of more than one word. Fill in each word in a straight line without crossing any black squares; when you're done, every square will be filled. GENRE has been entered for you.

ALOUD	IDLEST	NATIONAL	STAMPEDE
AMBITION	INFER	NOMADIC	TAMALE
ASSET	LATENT	OPPOSITE	TENTATIVE
BARGED	LEECH	PHOTOSTAT	THESPIAN
BROTH	LOUVER	PLAINTIFF	TRUE
BURST	MAPLE	ROTUNDA	USEFUL
CHANNEL	MOIST	SEPARATE	WOEFUL
CONSIDERABLE			
DIVERSION			
DOMAIN			
DROLL			
ENERGETIC			
EPITAPH			
FASTIDIOUS			
FIRST			
FRIVOLOUS			
GENRE			
GEODE			
GREEN			
HOIST			
HOSPITAL			

William Butler Yeats (1865-1939) is considered by many to be the greatest modern poet in the English language. His poetry reflected an interest in mysticism and a devotion to his native Ireland. Listed below are 32 of his poems.

ARROW (The)
A SONG
BLACK TOWER (The)
BYZANTIUM

DAWN (The)
DOLLS (The)
FRIENDS
GYRES (The)

LAPIS LAZULI
LULLABY
MAGI (The)
MASK (The)
MEMORY
MERMAID (The)
MERU
MOODS (The)
PARNELL
PEACE
PEACOCK (The)
REALISTS (The)
ROSE TREE (The)
SCHOLARS (The)
SECRET ROSE (The)
SPILT MILK
SPUR (The)
THERE
TO A SHADE
UNDER SATURN
WHAT THEN?
WHEEL (The)
WISDOM
WORDS

```
O M A S K L I M T L I P S Z
M L P B S W H E E L M N E G
E U G Y R E S W U E K E C N
R L W Z R Z J Z O N F H R R
M L Z A B O A Y P R S T E U
A A Y N S L M E I A R T T T
I B G T S O A E S P P A R A
D Y T I C C N C M I E H O S
S E P U E D H G K Q A W S R
L A R M S O N R H T C D E E
L Z P E L Z W I S D O M T D
O E D A H S A O T O C W R N
D F R D M T D H M L K R E U
D S D R O W S T S I L A E R
```

UNCLE SAM SEARCH

Here's a puzzle that honors our national figure, Uncle Sam. All of the four-letter words below can be made from the letters in UNCLE SAM. When you have circled all the entries, the leftover letters, when read from left to right starting at the top, will spell out a comment about Uncle Sam.

CALM	NAME	SCAM	SEAM
CAME	SALE	SCAN	SLAM
CANE	SAME	SCUM	SLUE
CASE	SANE	SEAL	SLUM
CAUL			
CLAM			
CLAN			
CLUE			
ELAN			
LACE			
LAME			
LANE			
LEAN			
LUNE			
MACE			
MALE			
MANE			
MAUL			
MEAL			
MEAN			
MULE			
MUSE			

```
U M N C C S L E S S C A
E L A N M A S M U L E V
S E R L S M N M U I A E
O L U N C E C E O F M M
T A U R U T A A M A C S
M H S E A L L N L O R E
C M O N N N M A S N L E
M Q A A L A E M C A S E
A U E L E E E E S L S N
N C C S E C M L E C N U
E C A M C A U E U N S L
I S U M U L S M S C A N
A T L A E X E F O R M S
```

Thomas Alva Edison was perhaps the greatest inventor in history. Read how, because of an absent-minded error, his own inventiveness turned against him.

Annoyed with people who took his favorite cigars, Thomas Edison had a special box of really foul-tasting and -smelling cigars made. But his wife accidentally packed that box when Edison went on a trip, and he ended up having to smoke them himself.

```
B A L Q U F O X O B T A H T
Z U C K L E R D W H O I X A
U T T C T S P E C I A L K S
C H Y H I W N Y D V F P R T
Z O E A I D E O S I I E W I
I M O N E S E N U R S C H N
Z A N D H E F N T X A O E G
K S U P L L Y A T V P G N I
O P Q U E G N I V A H I I Y
O T O S M O K E C O L O L C
T F M W S H P K D L R L Z Y
O I J I Z A E L E A A I Y M
H V D T T D V M E E M V T H
W E S H I A S S R A G I C E
```

Perhaps Thomas Edison imported his beloved cigars from Cuba, a country known for its fine quality cigars. This puzzle lists 32 cities in Cuba, including HAVANA, its capital.

ALQUIZAR

BÁGUANOS

BANES

BAUTA

BAYAMO

CAMAGÜEY

CÁRDENAS

CONDADO

CUETO

EL SANTO

ESMERALDA

GIBARA

GUANTÁNAMO

GUASIMAL

GÜINES

GUISA

HAVANA

HOLGUIN

MANACAS

MARIANAO

MARIEL

MARTI

MATANZAS

MAYARI

MINAS

MORÓN

PLACETAS

RODAS

SANTA CLARA

SOLA

YAGUAJAY

YARA

```
I O M A Y A B G G A Y R H M
H T O N I L Y E U G A M A C
I T R A M Q A T I S J T E T
S H O L G U I N S B A U T A
O A N T R I S A A N U W P R
N A D Y N Z C B Z V G L U A
A B N O M A N A T N A U G L
U A U A R R S I R C Y H C C
G U A S I M A L E D E U O A
A U O T A R C T E M E N Y T
B L I R A Y A M Y T D N O N
A M I N A S N M O A S R A A
L E S M E R A L D A R O E S
L B A N E S M O G I B A R A
```

TAIL TAG

Solve this puzzle by forming a chain of circled words in which the last letter of one word is the first letter of the next. The number in parentheses tells you the length of the word you're looking for. We have provided SLAP to start you off.

SLAP _____ (4)   _____ (5)   _____ (4)
P _____ (4)   _____ (6)   _____ (4)
_____ (6)   _____ (5)   _____ (5)
_____ (4)   _____ (7)   _____ (5)
_____ (4)   _____ (4)   _____ (4)
                                       _____ (5)
                                       _____ (5)
                                       _____ (6)
                                       _____ (5)
                                       _____ (4)
                                       _____ (6)
                                       _____ (8)
                                       _____ (4)
                                       _____ (4)
                                       _____ (5)
                                       _____ (4)
                                       _____ (5)
                                       _____ (6)
                                       _____ (4)
                                       _____ (5)
                                       _____ (4)
                                       _____ (4)
                                       _____ (6)
                                       _____ (6)
                                       _____ (5)
                                       _____ (4)
                                       _____ (4)
                                       _____ (6)
                                       _____ (5)

```
R Z Y H R E L A X I N G G M
E A W C E R M J K B Y A Z J
V V V A G R Z L C R A L O M
E Q Z E N Z O Q I U Q A I P
N E D L O G Z N T S R R R Z
H G I E L S N L S T T I X E
O Y Q L W N N I S E A M S G
O R I X V K N I R D Z W H N
P D N U O R I Z R T I Q Y A
A O L Q E S Y T Y G S R V R
N M K S W P Z Q T D P O L O
K X A E Y M J O N E L A G G
L R L R R U L E I W N G L L
E L E A D L X Z M A H S Y S
```

See word list at end of answer section.

If you're a collector of antique pottery, the names below may be familiar to you. Here are 29 companies that produced pottery, mainly during the 19th and early 20th centuries. Get cracking and see if you can find them all.

AREQUIPA

AVON

BUFFALO

CAMBRIDGE

CHELSEA

CLEWELL

COORS

COWAN

DEDHAM

GONDER

GOUDA

GRUEBY

HULL

MARBLEHEAD

NEWCOMB

NORSE

OHR

OWENS

PEWABIC

RED WING

ROSEVILLE

SHAWNEE

STANGL

TECO

VAN BRIGGLE

VANCE

WELLER

ZANE

ZANESVILLE

```
P I N E W C O M B C O O R S
S S G G A R E Q U I P A T R
G N A N H E D F F O R A E O
H O E I N S E T F F N R A S
U D N W N K D O A G M A W E
L A A D O C H E L S E A L V
L H N E E N A W O C N G O I
S L P R H R M M E E G K Y L
T E E N P E W A B I C B A L
E T O W E L L E R R E O D E
C C N H E T E B S U I H U I
O L N L R L N N R R S D O M
N O V A C A C G A A O C G O
E L L I V S E N A Z M N Y E
```

Alfred, Lord Tennyson wrote his *Idylls of the King* between 1859 and 1885. The 10 books of this series are made up of long narrative poems based on stories about King ARTHUR and the Knights of the Round Table. Hidden in the diagram below are the names of 30 characters that appear in this epic.

ABROSIUS   BALAN   BELLICENT

ANTON   BALIN   BORS

ARTHUR   BEDIVERE   DAGONET

DUBRIC

EDYRN

ELAINE

ENID

ETTARRE

GALAHAD

GARETH

GAWAIN

GERAINT

GUINEVERE

ISOLT

LANCELOT

LYNETTE

LYONORS

MARK

MERLIN

MODRED

PELLEAS

PERCIVALE

TRISTRAM

VIVIEN

```
H T I N C T R I S T R A M Q
G R S B I O N E T T E N Y L
K A O P E L L E A S N T B Y
A R L K F E A J C X I O M O
S B T A P C V B M I D N P N
E M R K H N R E G R L E Z O
T E N O G A D D U A R L C R
T R I L S L D H N C R I E S
A L A E K I T N I A R E G B
R I W R N R U V N B L X T Z
R N A D A I A S U R A A P H
E M G S G L A D L R Y O B N
V I V I E N K L D E R D O M
G U I N E V E R E V I D E B
```

In the Middle Ages, noblemen rode in carriages that bore a CREST or coat of arms. Different designs or emblems indicated rank or membership in the court of the monarchy. The word list below contains 30 examples of heraldic insignia.

BADGE

BARS

BEND

CHAPEAU

CHEVRON

CIRCLET

COLLAR

CORONET

CRESCENT

CREST

CROSS

CROWN

DRAGON

ESCUTCHEON

FESSE

FIELD

FLEUR-DE-LIS

GARLAND

GRILLE

HAWK

HELMET

LION

MOTTO

MURAL

SHIELD

SIGNET

STANDARD

STAR

SUPPORTER

WREATH

```
D M S N W O R C H N E B O B
I O D H R A L L O C R E N E
S T L R I A D E N R L I O N
I T E M L E H T O T O S R D
L O I O H C L O G C E N V O
E R F S T A N D A R D K E C
D A H U S T E T R E C W H T
R T C C S H G S D S N A C H
U S E I O A R A S C P H K S
E E G T R T I W R E A T H I
L O D L C C L N A N F S E G
F L A R U M L U I T O E V N
A N B U C S E E R B A R S E
D O S U P P O R T E R C R T
```

When you look for the terms in this puzzle, you'll find that each bends at an angle and none of the terms overlap. SPATULA is outlined to show you. Turn on the TIMER and see how fast you can find the 23 types of kitchen helpers hidden below.

```
W A S H E R R R E T E M O M
H S G T I M E I L L E T P R
S B T E V I R T K V C O E E
I R A R E C I P S S T V E H
D E C E R M I L L B A R F T
J C K P C P R E S S L E F R
N I I P W I S P A T U X O E
D C R E S N L S D L C I C N
E H E P A T I R C O R A M E
M R D L B G E P A M O C N P
A O N E L B T R G G L I E O
K T R E N I A R Y N L U R R
E I T O A S T E T D I J L H
R S S E R I E R M S E L D A
```

BASTER
BLENDER
CAN OPENER
COFFEE POT
DICER
DISHWASHER
GARLIC PRESS
ICE MAKER
JUICER
LADLE
MIXER
MOLDS
PEPPER MILL
ROLLING PIN
ROTISSERIE
SKILLET
SPATULA
SPICE RACK
STRAINER
THERMOMETER
TIMER
TOASTER
TRIVETS

Get with it and search for words containing the consecutive letters "IT."
There are 50 words of four letters or longer.

YOUR WORD LIST

```
R V O R B F Y T T I K E R M
T E X I T S T C Q U T I E G
I R T S P L I T O I V T T R
A E Q I Z T L H C T I H I E
G T R U A P I T Y L T G L H
P I X D I W B X F N A I A T
T O E V I T A L T E M B D I
R L L N Z T E D I T I O N W
E Q U I O S C T M T N T H K
S S E N T I W H I I H I C N
P I E I M E T C L M T E G H
I O T G K S P I T E O I X T
T L I E T I F T U O P F N Y
E O R B I T V Y Z T I L G K
```

See word list at end of answer section.

John Adams was on the committee that adopted and signed the Declaration of Independence. He believed that the day the Declaration was signed would be "celebrated by succeeding generations as the great anniversary." How he believed it should be celebrated is quoted below from a letter to his wife in 1776. When you have circled all the entries, the leftover letters will spell out another John Adams saying.

It ought
to be
commemorated

as the
day of
deliverance,

by solemn
acts of
devotion
to God
Almighty.
It ought
to be
celebrated
with
pomp
and
parade,
with
shows,
games,
sports,
guns,
bells,
bonfires,
and
illuminations,
from
one end
of this
continent
to the
other.

```
T D E T A R B E L E C E S M
H E W I T H C H F A H N O P
D E V O T I O N O T O R P S
E D A R A P N I S I F N I E
H G U N S S T A T O T H E S
E T A O D F I A C S T D A O
C R I M C I N E A F N P L S
N E T W E I E M O E D O M E
A H Y S M S N I E I A M I R
R T S U H T T N H L Y P G I
E O L D E O O H D E O N H F
V L D O U T W T G N F S T N
I O F G G O O S O U A V Y O
L E H O R B N S T R O P S B
E T M T E E B E L L S T E N
D E T A R O M E M M O C I T
```

Scan the grid in all directions for 54 familiar five-letter words, arranged in pairs. Each word in a pair crosses its partner through the center letter, forming either a "+" or an "x" shape. One pair has been circled to start you off.

YOUR WORD LIST

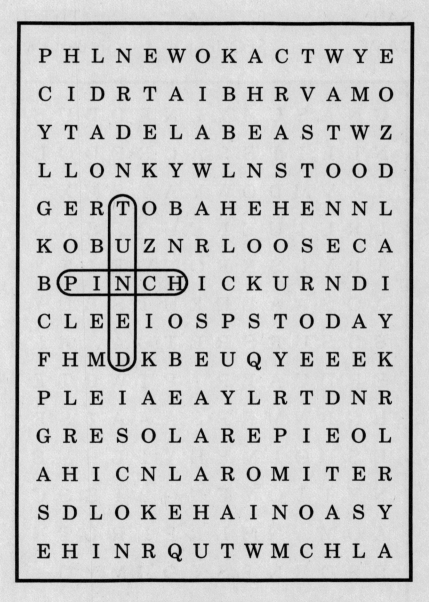

See word list at end of answer section.

SOMEWHERE in SPAIN, a SUNNY SUMMER day SUDDENLY became STORMY. Sing along while you search for 38 songs that all start with the letter "S."

SACRED

SAILING

SALLY

SAME

SANDY

SARA

SEE SAW

SEQUEL

SERENADE

SHADRACK

SHATTERED

SH-BOOM

SHILO

SHIPS

SHOUT

SIBONEY

SIMILAU

SINCERELY

SING

SLEEP

SMILE

SOLITAIRE

SOMEWHERE

SOON

SORRY

SOULS

SPAIN

S'POSIN'

STAND

STAY

STILL

STORMY

STRUT

SUDDENLY

SUMMER

SUNNY

SUSAN

SWAY

```
G N A S U S Y L N E D D U S
N L L I T S S A C R E D O U
I Y V M D O W Y A T S M X N
L R L I U E L E U Q E S N N
I R Y L S K R O N W E I T Y
A O S A A E H E H I S B U Y
S S S U R S R E T O A S R L
E H D U A F R I P T W P T E
R G B N M E P S A A A I S R
E S D O L M E H Y T L H M E
N Y T I O Y E N O B I S S C
A O M A N M L R P L R L T N
D S O G N I S T O R M Y O I
E M A S S D K C A R D A H S
```

. . . AND SONGSTERS ——————————— 112

Now we have singers whose last names start with the letter "S." We're SURE you'll be SHARP finding them all.

SADE

SANG
(Samantha)

SAYER (Leo)

SCAGGS (Boz)

SHANICE

SHANNON

SHARP
(Dee Dee)

SHERMAN
(Bobby)

SHORE (Dinah)

SIMON (Carly)

SIMONE (Nina)

SINATRA (Frank)

SLEDGE (Percy)

SMITH (Bessie)

SNOW
(Phoebe)

SPECTOR
(Ronnie)

SPRINGFIELD
(Dusty)

STAFFORD (Jo)

STANSFIELD (Lisa)

STARR (Kay)

STATON (Candi)

STIGERS (Curtis)

STREISAND (Barbra)

SUMMER (Donna)

SURE (Al B.)

SWEAT (Keith)

SWEET (Rachel)

SYLVIA

```
E R O H S S R E G I T S A
R G R M M H E C S W E A T
R T O I G T A I S S R Y D
A O T S A D E N T A Z E R
T H C A D N U A N T N R O
S H E R M A N H V O J G F
S T P Y L S W S M S N Q F
H G S A F I H I W O N S A
A W G I O E S N T L S U T
R K E A G R I A E R U S S
P L Q D C T T T N I M I T
D T E E W S R R W J M E R
Z L S Y L V I A F O E M
S C D L E I F G N I R P S
```

129

The Soap Box Derby is an annual event in which children race homemade vehicles down an inclined raceway. There are different kinds of go-carts, such as ENDURO carts (raced on paved roads) and SPEEDWAY carts (raced on dirt or clay surfaces). See how long it takes to cross the finish line and find the 35 terms associated with go-cart racing.

AXLE	BRAKE	CHASSIS
BATTERY	BUMPER	CLUTCH
BELT	CHAIN	ENDURO
		EXHAUST
		FAIRING
		FINS
		FLAG
		FRAME
		FUEL
		GAUGE
		GEARS
		HEADER
		MOTOCROSS
		NOMEX
		PITS
		POINTS
		PULLEY
		ROLL BAR
		SLICKS
		SPEEDWAY
		SPOILER
		SPRINT
		STARTER
		STRUT
		TACHOMETER
		TIRES
		TRACK
		TREAD
		WHEELBASE

```
A S S O R C O T O M P F X D
I B C T D R U Q T V S I E C
H T S U A H X E M O N N T E
G L F Y E R O P G W D S L S
J E Y R E T T A B U D X L B
L B K G M L N E R R A Z A E
P O I N T S L O R T E G S F
C H A I N N L U J I R H L G
S B R R E L I O P S T A I H
I E R I B A S R A E G L C M
S Z Y A W D E E P S F T K K
S T R F K P U D T S U O S N
A F R A M E S A B L E E H W
H D C U B W V E C S L P Q R
C Y B X T A C H O M E T E R
```

From Gilbert STUART's portraits to Andy WARHOL's pop art, American art includes a wide range of styles. Listed here are 34 noted artists.

ALBERS (Josef)
BELLOWS (George)
CASSATT (Mary)
CHASE (William)
COLE (Thomas)
COPLEY (John Singleton)
DAVIS (Stuart)
DINE (Jim)
DOVE (Arthur)
EAKINS (Thomas)
EARL (Ralph)
FEKE (Robert)
GRAVES (Morris)
HASSAM (Childe)
HICKS (Edward)
HOMER (Winslow)
LA FARGE (John)
LUKS (George)
MARIN (John)
MORSE (Samuel)
MOSES (Grandma)
REMINGTON (Frederic)
ROCKWELL (Norman)
SARGENT (John Singer)

SHINN (Everett)
SLOAN (John)
STILL (Clyfford)
STUART (Gilbert)
TRUMBULL (John)

WARHOL (Andy)
WEBER (Max)
WEST (Benjamin)
WHISTLER (James)
WYETH (Andrew)

```
N W R E L T S I H W Q M S S
K N Y T S A R G E N T K W C
G L I E C P E Z R S C O L R
W M L H T Y B S T I L L T E
L O A M S H L Q H L C O T M
L S R A E E A R E M O H A I
E E L S W W E B E R P R S N
W S J S E L O C L F L L S G
K R R A O S X A S E E T A T
C O N H N E F L N T Y K C O
O M R I D A V I S K U L E N
R A K L R J D O S E V A R G
W A T G L A L Q D L R T R C
E W E T R U M B U L L C L T
```

MATH FUN

Here's a puzzle of a different sort. First complete each of the simple arithmetic problems in order, from left to right. Then write the answer in the space provided and search for that word in the diagram. We've done number 7 to show you what we mean. Note: If you're looking for six, be careful not to circle part of sixty or sixteen. Answers may be repeated; look for each one in the diagram.

1. $49 + 34 - 21 = \underline{\hspace{1cm}}$

2. $88 \times 2 \div 16 = \underline{\hspace{1cm}}$

3. $14 + 24 + 59 = \underline{\hspace{1cm}}$

4. $144 \div 2 \div 6 = \underline{\hspace{1cm}}$

5. $18 \times 6 \div 36 = \underline{\hspace{1cm}}$

6. $21 + 15 - 29 = \underline{\hspace{1cm}}$

7. $25 \times 6 \div 30 = \underline{\text{FIVE}}$

8. $38 - 7 + 20 = \underline{\hspace{1cm}}$

9. $6 \times 21 - 103 = \underline{\hspace{1cm}}$

10. $38 - 12 - 19 = \underline{\hspace{1cm}}$

11. $7 \times 8 + 35 = \underline{\hspace{1cm}}$

12. $15 \times 8 \div 2 = \underline{\hspace{1cm}}$

13. $78 - 63 - 13 = \underline{\hspace{1cm}}$

14. $6 \times 15 \div 15 = \underline{\hspace{1cm}}$

15. $13 + 38 + 46 = \underline{\hspace{1cm}}$

16. $44 - 15 - 17 = \underline{\hspace{1cm}}$

17. $49 \times 4 \div 28 = \underline{\hspace{1cm}}$

18. $16 + 48 + 31 = \underline{\hspace{1cm}}$

19. $46 \times 8 \div 4 = \underline{\hspace{1cm}}$

20. $21 + 38 - 56 = \underline{\hspace{1cm}}$

21. $12 \times 24 \div 48 = \underline{\hspace{1cm}}$

22. $16 + 16 + 18 = \underline{\hspace{1cm}}$

23. $9 \times 12 \div 36 = \underline{\hspace{1cm}}$

24. $42 + 29 - 51 = \underline{\hspace{1cm}}$

25. $15 \times 15 \div 45 = \underline{\hspace{1cm}}$

26. $24 + 14 - 32 = \underline{\hspace{1cm}}$

27. $13 \times 5 - 19 = \underline{\hspace{1cm}}$

28. $9 + 18 + 33 = \underline{\hspace{1cm}}$

29. $15 \times 26 + 512 = \underline{\hspace{1cm}}$

30. $28 \times 3 \div 12 = \underline{\hspace{1cm}}$

31. $42 - 28 - 12 = \underline{\hspace{1cm}}$

32. $11 + 11 + 28 = \underline{\hspace{1cm}}$

33. $9 \times 9 - 52 = \underline{\hspace{1cm}}$

34. $32 \times 3 \div 12 = \underline{\hspace{1cm}}$

35. $12 + 50 - 29 = \underline{\hspace{1cm}}$

```
F I F T Y O T T T A S U N N
I N I W O W F T H R E E I O
F O V E E T W O I R V N N T
T W E N T Y T H R E E I E Y
Y T T T O T O T T T N E T R
O Y N Y T X I S Y A F Y O
N T S N S I T S T S I S F F
E E A I E S E H H F E L I E
V N X N X V I L R R E V V X
E I E E E T E X E E L E O
S N I N E T Y S E V E N E N
T A G O W N I W T W E L V E
E O H O N I N E T Y O N E E
O W T D E R D N U H E N I N
```

See answers at end of answer section.

"TEE" TIME

Even though golf has been around since the 14th century, the practice of using tees was not a part of the game until the 1920s. Here is the story of how golfers began "teeing off."

Golf courses	to avoid	champion,
once had	getting	used
tee boxes	his hands	the new
containing	dirty,	tee in
a bucket of water	Dr. William	exhibitions
and some	Lowell,	across the
sand.	a New Jersey	United States.
Players had	dentist,	The idea
to make	invented	caught on
their	a wooden	quickly.
own tees	peg called	Soon
by wetting	the "Reddy Tee."	the sand
sand and	Professional	and water
shaping it	golfer	pail
with their	Walter	became
fingers.	Hagen, a	relics of
In order	British Open	the past.

134

```
Y I N V E N T E D S D N A H S I H F L T
G N I N I A T N O C N C A U G H T O N E
T I G N I P A H S W A L T E R J H S R C
D E N T I S T H E I D E A I E M A C E B
W E A S K L U X M P N H S R E G N I F Y
G T U N I T E D S T A T E S Y S E L L W
B E R O E L A N O I S S E F O R P E O E
L C T I A G R M P H L S T O L A O R G T
D I V T Y Z A R E D R O N I K N H M R T
A L W I I K O H M U Y R W Y C E S A T I
H R E B E N O V O T T C O E E A I I L N
S S N I Q Y G C S K R A H T L N T L C G
R I E H T U F R D A I A Y I E L I L T N
E U H X W L I C N B D D M D U A R I H E
Y S T E O A G C A L D I O N P S B W E O
A T Y G A B U C K E T O F W A T E R S P
L S P L Y R E S R L W T O A V O I D A T
P E G C A L L E D A Y E S R E J W E N A
N O I P M A H C T U R M T Y L S K O D L
C I H W I T H T H E I R E T A W D N A Y
```

The military tank was first developed in Great Britain. Its main features are its caterpillar traction and invulnerability to many offensive weapons. The British tanks in the word list are marked with an asterisk (*); all the other tanks are American-made.

ACHILLES*   AVENGER*   CAVALIER*

ADDER   BADGER   COMET*

ALECTO*   BARON*   CRAB*

ARCHER*   CARROT*   CRIB

                CRUSADER*

                DOZER

                FLAIL

```
R A B D I R B Y H G H B S I
T E M O C E W B P R A M E J
C D I E F G V S I D L K X M
L I A L F N R S G R A N T G
P T O N A E Q E N B C A O N
D O Z E R V R A P A O M N I
L R J A M A A R Q R K R N H
K R I D A L E C T O P E E S
T A C L L E H H H N R H S R
H C G I D N Y E X I W S A E
G G R T B T C R A O L W D P
F O V A L I E N T N Y L D T
G R A M B N C R U S A D E R
E F D T S E I R P Z V U R S
```

FROG*

GOAT*

GORILLA

GRANT

HELLCAT

HYBRID

MATILDA

ONION*

PERSHING

PRAM*

PRIEST*

PSY-WAR

SEXTON*

SHERMAN

SNAKE*

TOPEE

VALENTINE*

VALIENT*

The 1944 film *Hollywood Canteen* was an all-star salute to the movie industry's part in the war effort. The cast included many of Hollywood's biggest stars, performing their classic routines. The list below consists of the names of some of those stars.

ANDREWS (Sisters)

BENNY (Jack)

BISHOP (Julie)

BROWN (Joe E.)

CANTOR (Eddie)

CARSON (Jack)

CLARK (Dane)

CRAWFORD (Joan)

DANTINE (Helmut)

DAVIS (Bette)

EMERSON (Faye)

GARFIELD (John)

GORDON (Mary)

GREENSTREET (Sydney)

HALE (Alan)

HENREID (Paul)

HUTTON (Robert)

LESLIE (Joan)

LORRE (Peter)

LUPINO (Ida)

MALONE (Dorothy)

MORAN (Dolores)

MORGAN (Dennis)

PAIGE (Janis)

PARKER (Eleanor)

ROGERS (Roy)

SCOTT (Zachary)

STANWYCK (Barbara)

STEVENS (Craig)

TOWNSEND (Colleen)

TRIGGER

WYMAN (Jane)

```
J T E E R T S N E E R G S
D L E I F R A G L B X R S
H A L E E L N N I Z E D N
O K N K L O E S D G J R E
N R R T S H S O R E O V
I A J R I O E R L G E F E
P L A Q P N M Z G I N W T
U C H E N R E I D A E A S
L O R R E W R J G M G R T
M D X J O T S R Z O I C A
B A H U T T O N R R A Y N
R V L O T M N D R A P A W
O I C O Z M O A V N M W Y
W S B E N N Y X C Y J M C
N J Z D N E S N W O T A K
```

The Chinese used fireworks to frighten off evil spirits and to celebrate special occasions. They called their bamboo firecrackers "arrows of flying fire"; how they invented fireworks is explained below. Today, the art of pyrotechnics is led by the renowned Grucci family. When you have circled all the entries, the leftover letters will spell out a comment about great inventions.

In the tenth century, a Chinese cook invented fireworks with three elements that were common in Chinese kitchens. He mixed pickling salt (saltpeter), a fire intensifier (sulfur), and charred coal (charcoal), and created history's first man-made explosion of sparks.

```
T H C R E T E P T L A S T E
G R E E E A W T I N T H E E
S S E T N I O E D S A L T L
A Y D B T T F F R T D O C R
S R A H A V U I S E E I O E
N O M M O C F R S P T L O X
S T N E M E L E Y N A N K P
N S A G P A N W I O E R N L
E I M C F I C O C V R T K O
H H E I H H C R H N C H N S
C T R C A I A K I T O R N I
T E N R O H N S L I N E S O
I I R T C A D E X I M E H N
K E O R U F L U S M N O T R
D I N V E N T E D E R G O W
```

What quote from Henry David Thoreau describing the flight of a particular bird is hidden in the diagram? To find out, circle the 40 types of birds below. The unused letters will spell out the answer.

AUK	ORIOLE	QUAIL	SWAN
BLACKBIRD	OWL	RAVEN	TANAGER
BLUEBIRD	PENGUIN	ROBIN	TERN
BUNTING	PETREL	SPARROW	WARBLER
CARDINAL	PIGEON	STORK	WREN
CHAT			
CRANE			
CURLEW			
DUCK			
EAGLE			
EIDER			
FLICKER			
GRACKLE			
GREBE			
GROUSE			
HAWK			
HERON			
JAY			
JUNCO			
KEA			
KILLDEER			
LARK			
LINNET			
LOON			
MYNAH			

```
H A N Y M T B U N T I N G Q
H E W A R B L E R E E E U B
L C R L U N A E B R I A N W
E H L O O N C E W I I D R O
R A V E N T K I L L D E E R
T T G F R E B D A K O C T R
E I A L A N I D R A C R R A
P I W I E N R P K E N A U P
S O G C T I D E N H U K R S
K E R K B L S N G A J K O G
Y C O E B E R G H A W K B O
N C U R L E W U Y H N S I I
S L S D E L O I R O B A N A
B C E K C R A N E K R O T S
```

To solve this puzzle, you must first fill in the circles with letters from the words below. The number in parentheses after a word indicates how many circles to fill in order to find that word in the diagram. When you have solved the puzzle correctly, the circled letters will reveal an historical event that occurred on September 17, 1787.

ABSENTIA (3)   COQUET (2)   ESCROW (2)   HOMAGE (3)

ANALOGY (2)   DECOCT (2)   FARO (2)   HOUSE (1)

ATTACH (2)   DISCO (2)   FINANCE (2)   IBIS (2)

CITY (1)   ENOUGH (2)   GENIE (2)   IMPOUND (2)

COCOA (2)   ESCORT (2)   HOGAN (2)   INURE (2)

KINGDOM (3)

KNIGHT (2)

LONG (1)

MITT (2)

NAIVE (3)

NIGHT (3)

NUBBIER (3)

NYLON (2)

ORBIT (2)

POLITE (3)

SMUG (2)

STATUE (2)

SWAN (2)

TONGUE (3)

TREBLE (1)

VILIFY (2)

WHITEN (2)

WIZEN (2)

```
N E O I O W F E L B O R T E
V T C H O E I K Q V N A K O
E O T H O I O K O J O P M C
S B L A A I A A U N U U D O
U R M I N A O A L O O Y E R
O O R A O A C R H E H D C O
O U C E W Y E O N O O C O A
O A B O E N O O A O A N C M
E Y I C I I E B N Q G T O Y
Z B L R L D L B E O T A O S
O M P O U N D U E E R I I A
W X P W N L O O G T C E M Z
```

There are about 300 species of hummingbirds, all of which are attracted to nectar-bearing plants. If you'd like to see hummingbirds in your yard, we've listed 31 plants, common to the southwest, that you can plant.

ABELIA

BEEBALM

BOUVARDIA

CANNA

CIGAR PLANT

CITRUS

COLUMBINE

CORAL (vine)

DIANTHUS

FIREBUSH

FOUR O'CLOCK

GERANIUM

HIBISCUS

IMPATIENS

JASMINE

LANTANA

LILY

MYRTLE (crepe)

NICOTIANA

PEACH (blossom)

PEAR (blossom)

PENSTEMON

PETUNIA

PHLOX

PLUM (blossom)

POINCIANA

SALVIA

TRUMPET (vine)

VERBENA

VITEX

YUCCA

```
S U H T N A I D R A V U O B
N I C O T I A N A T N A L C
E T V S H H P P N Q G S J A
I C I K U H S A L E B U A N
T V T M L R L U R U K C S N
A S E O L P T A B C M S M A
P A X R R A N I O E Y I I N
M L C A B I B L C R R B N A
I V G C U E C E W Y T I E I
H I L M U O N B E P L H F C
C A A N R Y F A X B E I J N
A T R U M P E T U N I A L I
E N O M E T S N E P V L R O
P F C O L U M B I N E M P P
```

The text below was taken from the King James version of the Holy Bible. You'll find it in Psalm 81, verses 1 through 3.

```
J O E T H E N E W M O O N Q
T H E T I M B R E L E Q A U
G N I S N L J R Y A U M N I
N W U T O A U Q N S Q O I Y
F M Q W H O S D U P I U R T
R O U J N E B A Q S Q E R H
G O D O U R R F E N T U E T
A P P O I N T E D L M Q P G
L E X N G S H A A P P U R N
O I G B O T J S E U Q E A E
U B N L O A P T K K N U H R
D Q E T C E I D A Z A T Q T
U M N O H N E A M Q P T O S
N U B T N E J Y L U F Y O J
```

Sing aloud unto God our strength: make a joyful noise unto the God of Jacob. Take a psalm, and bring hither the timbrel, the pleasant harp with the psaltery. Blow up the trumpet in the new moon, in the time appointed, on our solemn feast day.

To solve this puzzle, fill in the circles with letters to form words from the list below. The number in parentheses after each word indicates how many circles to fill in order to find that word in the diagram. When you've solved the puzzle correctly, the circled letters will reveal the title of a book by a pioneer in public speaking.

ACACIA (3)
AJAR (2)
ASPIRE (2)
BRAVO (2)
BULGE (1)
CLIENT (2)
EQUINE (2)
FANTAIL (3)
FORFEIT (3)
FROWN (2)
FRUMPY (2)
FUDGE (2)
FUNNY (2)
HEIR (2)
INDIAN (3)
IN-LAW (2)
INURE (2)
JOLT (1)
KILN (2)
LINGO (2)
LOST (2)
LOVELY (2)
NEXT (1)
NODE (2)
OFTEN (2)
OWNING (2)
OXEN (1)
PLEASE (1)
PLOY (1)
PONE (2)
PUNT (2)
RODEO (2)
RULER (2)
SEDAN (2)
SOLVE (2)
SOOTHE (2)
SPIGOT (4)

SUEDE (2)
SWEETLY (2)
TONGUED (3)
TWEET (2)
TWINGE (1)

UNCAP (3)
UNCLE (2)
VALUE (1)
VEST (1)
WEAR (2)

```
E O T O O S O E E O L Y C
F Q E F V G E E T O X E N L
U J T I A A N R G O A L N O
O E O O F E O T N I O W O
O O U O B A P P L I X N Q N
Y E O E U O J S N N P U G T
Y E G E E U L O V G I Z I E
O O E O A I O N O O W O R O
B U O G E E E N E C T U A R
T I O P S R O L O R A O V U
K W V N T R G N T N T O U M
T S O V E S N L C A O A A O
H X L O V L O S I L C O Z Y
T O Y Y T J T O P L O A S E
```

The *Fiesta de San Fermín* is held each July in Pamplona, Spain. The nine-day festival is highlighted by the well-known "running of the bulls" through the narrow, winding streets. Read on to learn how bulls respond to the color red.

Contrary to popular belief, bulls are not uniquely agitated by the color red. All cattle are almost color-blind, and bulls react to red the same as any other bright color. The reason bullfighters use red capes is for audience appeal, because red reacts most quickly on the human optic nerve.

```
M T R Y L E U Q I N U A N O
B O E O I M U C O L O R R W
E H S T F A Q S E H T Y B E
L S T T M S A U D I E N C E
I L U C E E I F I D N A O S
E L G A R H R E A C T S Y R
F U M E C T R G R T K A A E
S B H R L E I D O G L L V T
O T E O D T B N L P A R Y H
W D Y R A R T N O C E R E G
O E L T I E P A C N P O E I
N T E G D D U O C A P E S F
T D H N D S L I B L A L L L
H T I E E O T S O M L A L L
E L E S R P H U M A N A U U
B T O P O P U L A R U S B B
```

On December 17, 1903, Orville WRIGHT made the first successful airplane flight. Since that time, John GLENN, Jr. was the first to orbit the earth three times and Neil ARMSTRONG was the first to walk on the moon. Search below for 39 pioneers in air and space. The unused letters will spell two more "frequent flyers."

ARMSTRONG (Neil)
ARNOLD ("Hap")
BEECH (Olive)
BOEING (William)
BORMAN (Frank)
BOYD (Albert)
BYRD (Richard)
CESSNA (Clyde)
COCHRAN (Jacqueline)
CURTISS (Glenn)
DRAPER (Charles)
EAKER (Ira)
EARHART (Amelia)
ELY (Eugene)
FOKKER (Anthony)
FOSS (Joseph)
GLENN (John Jr.)
GRISSOM (Virgil)
GROSS (Robert)
HUGHES (Howard)
LEAR (William)
LE MAY (Curtis)
LINDBERG (Charles)
LINK (Edwin)
LUKE (Frank Jr.)
MARTIN (Glenn)
PIPER (William)
POST (Wiley)
READ (Albert)

RICKENBACKER (Edward)
ROGERS (Will)
RYAN (Claude)
SCHIRRA (Walter)
SHEPARD (Alan Jr.)

STAPP (John)
TAYLOR (Charles)
WADE (Leigh)
WRIGHT (Orville)
YEAGER (Charles)

```
A S R O L Y A T R A H R A E
C E S S N A L L S B C L P F
U H C O E R E L Y R E R O O
R G H B F M D R A P E H S K
T U I O A S D E A K B G T K
I H R Y N T L R C W L O O E
S C R D M R N A D R A P E R
S N A M R O B O E I N G L P
M N K H L N S K E G E D I P
E A J D E G U S O H R P N A
A Y R K H L N T I T E O K T
K R C T Y E A G E R O D S S
E I W L I N D B E R G E A S
R E A D R N A R H C O C S W
```

Your TALENT for solving Tanglewords will REVEAL itself if you make a HABIT of solving these puzzles.

ADVOCATED CHARACTER GARNISH LEGISLATE
ANISETTE DATED GENIE LIGHT
AUTHORED DISTRIBUTED GEOMETRIC MAGNESIUM
BALLERINA DRAM GIGANTIC MASON
BARITONE ELBOW HABIT MISTER
BRAWL ENDEMIC INTERRUPT MOTTLED
CABARET ENTER ISSUE OBSTREPEROUS
OSTEOPATHY
PASTURE
PRAISE
REALISTIC
RENDER
REVEAL
SMUG
STEATITE
STRAIT
TALENT
TEASPOON
TRADE
WITHIN

A TRIBE of MISSHAPEN and GLUM thugs pulled off a JEWEL CAPER. With RELUCTANCE they ABANDONed the VEHICLE containing their BAGGAGE and hurried to LEAGUE night festivities at the local bowling alley. You don't have to PIECE this story together. Just enjoy solving the WHOLE puzzle.

ABANDON	MISSHAPEN	RELIEVE	TOGGLE
ATRIA	NIECE	RELUCTANCE	TRIBE
BAGGAGE	NOTED	RETROSPECT	VEHICLE
BARREL	NYLON	SINGE	VOTE
BENIGN	PIECE	SMOOTH	WHETSTONE
BRINE	PRACTICAL	SUBMERGE	WHOLE
CAPER	PRELATE	THIAMINE	WINCE
DART			
DOGGEREL			
EDIBLE			
ELEMENTARY			
FAILURE			
FIANCÉ			
FLAMBÉ			
GLUM			
GUNBOAT			
HUMANLY			
INTEGRATE			
JEWEL			
LAMINATED			
LAYER			
LEAGUE			
MAGNOLIA			
MARMOT			

According to legend, Saint CHRISTOPHER would carry people across rivers when there were no bridges. Because of this, he is regarded as the patron saint of travelers. Find CHRISTOPHER and 27 other saints associated with specific groups or occupations hidden below.

AGATHA (nurses)

ARNOLD (millers)

BARBARA (miners)

BONIFACE (wheelwrights)

CATHARINE (scholars)

CECILIA (musicians)

CHRISTOPHER (travelers)

CLEMENT (tanners)

COSME (doctors)

CRISPIN (shoemakers)

ELOY (goldsmiths)

GORE (potters)

HUBERT (hunters)

JAMES (netmakers)

JOHN (freemen)

JOSEPH (carpenters)

LOUIS (barbers)

LUKE (painters)

MARTHA (housewives)

MATTHEW (tax collectors)

NICHOLAS (children)

PAUL (upholsterers)

PETER (locksmiths)

PIERAN (tinsmiths)

RAPHAEL (pilgrims)

STEPHEN (weavers)

VALENTINE (sweethearts)

WINIFRED (bakers)

```
J E N I T N E L A V M N Y K
R D H V W R N C L U A P O N
E G O R E E H E A R N O L D
H N J L H M Z C E F Y F E Q
P X I P T A N I P S I R C B
O C E R T R P L T H S N L A
T T L Q A T C I E A K B O R
S R S E M H J A L A C R U B
I E E W M A T O G O H N I A
R T M B D E H A S A L P S R
H E A G U C N M C E T U A A
C P J Z I H E T Y K P H K R
L W I N I F R E D N X H A E
```

Here is an interesting story that explains an often-heard phrase. Take a break from balancing the budget and enjoy solving the puzzle.

When you say you are trying to make both ends meet, you are using a nautical phrase that began centuries ago. Frugal sailing ship owners, rather than replace damaged rope, had the frayed ends spliced together. They saved money by "making both ends meet."

```
M E K A M O T S P L I C E D
E W J L N H Y D H N R O X E
E R Y A Z A V N S Y A T G G
T D A G S P U E S A R H P A
E R A U O Y I T Z Y D V T M
R E O R O R T H I M E E T A
E Y H F U Y O N S C Y N Y D
P B O T H Z G P B S A V E D
L Q N S D N E O E G R L N H
A E N E I A T Y E T F Q O U
C M S L H H H B E M H G M S
E T I D J W E R E H T A R I
Q A O W N E R S W R T N T N
S L M R H E B Y M A K I N G
```

KISS ME, YOU FOOL

The *Guinness Book of Records* has recorded the most kisses by one person and the longest kiss in movies. Interestingly enough, the longest movie kiss belongs to a woman who was once married to Ronald Reagan. When you have circled all the entries, the leftover letters will spell out a quote by Shakespeare on kisses.

The most	And the
kisses	longest kiss
were from	allowed
John	by movie
McPherson.	censors
In nineteen	was
eighty-five	three
he kissed	minutes
four	and five
thousand	seconds
four	between
hundred	Regis
forty-	Toomey
four	and Jane
women in	Wyman
England	in *You're*
within	*in the*
eight hours.	*Army Now.*

```
S N E E T E N I N N I T T W B E
I W Y A R M Y N O W W S A E R V
G Y T S E C O N D S O S T U H I
E M R E I P K I S M M W O S Y F
R A O F V H O U E T E F A K E Y
L N F O O E I H C E N S O R S T
H O A U M R T S N K I S S E S H
E I N R Y S S E T U N I M R D G
K N D G B O B M E O T H U E E I
I Y J D E N W N O H O O O V W E
S O A E T S G I R R H M I J O A
S U N R T L T E T T F F E F L N
E R E D A E E K H H D E O Y L D
D E I N T H E G I N I U R R A T
T H D U A N I Y A S R N O E U H
G I V H E E T H O U S A N D W E
```

Swamps cover approximately 100,000 square miles of the US. Much of this area is in the eastern part of the country, where swamps formed when glaciers retreated, leaving areas with poor drainage. Florida's EVERGLADES is one of the best-known swamps, and is one of 21 hidden below.

```
S S S E R P Y C T A E R G T
E N E E E K O N E F E K O H
D V C K B J E Q U M L I U O
A A E L A R U E M I A T H N
L Y I R E L O I N E E R G E
G A S K G B P I A K A L A Y
Y L M D U L J M C W C E A I
R A Y O O I A I A O J B T S
R F Y I E S H D N W S N G L
E A W M A T Y G E D S R R A
B H E I G E A L O S E E M N
N C H I I R E O L A M S I D
A T B H E H W I T O O E N A
R A A E H U M B O L D T G H
C R A N E S V I L L E E O A
```

ALAKAI (HI)

ATCHAFALAYA (LA)

BAYOU BOEUF (LA)

BIG THICKET (TX)

BLISTER (WV)

CONGAREE (SC)

CRANBERRY
GLADES (WV)

CRANESVILLE
(MD, WV)

DISMAL (VA, NC)

DOLLY SODS (WV)

EVERGLADES (FL)

GREAT (RI)

GREAT CYPRESS
(DE)

GREEN (FL)

HONEY ISLAND
(MS, LA)

HUMBOLDT (NV)

LARUE (MS)

MINGO (MS)

OKEFENOKEE (GA)

SWAMP LAKES
(TX, LA)

WOODS BAY (SC)

A trip through the Everglades reveals a rich diversity of flora. In this lush landscape are dim tree swamps with matted vines, still water, and a profusion of orchids; wet prairies and marshes thick with rushes; savannas set with clumps of palms; and low stone outcrops bearing both evergreens and tropical trees. Circle the varied wildlife along the way as you paddle through the puzzle.

ASH
BALD CYPRESS
BUTTERFLY
  ORCHID
CABBAGE PALM
CHERRY PALM
COCO PALM
CROTON
GHOST ORCHID
MANGROVE
MAPLE
MOONVINE
OAK
PARADISE
PEPEROMIA
PINE
POND APPLE
POP ASH
ROYAL PALM
SATINLEAF
SAWGRASS
SAW PALMETTO
VANILLA ORCHID
WAX MYRTLE
WILD COFFEE
WILLOW

```
B D N A C R E E L P A M V B
A Z I O M O O N V I N E A U
L M V H T X C J M B E E N T
D O I L C O W O L L I W I T
C T C H E R R Y P A L M L E
Y T U Y H E O C L A P M L R
P E P S P S A T I N L E A F
R M O E T I W E S A I M O L
E L P P A D N O P O L A R Y
S A A M W A X E J F H N C O
S P S S A R G W A S O G H R
O W H M L A P L A Y O R I C
O A N X B P A L O M R O D H
V S K B K O R F F E E V K I
B L A W I L D C O F F E E D
U C A K E L T R Y M X A W S
```

WORKS OF NORMAN ROCKWELL ———————————

American artist Norman Rockwell (1894-1978) gained great popularity as a cover illustrator for "The Saturday Evening Post." His paintings, 35 of which are listed below, capture the warmth and humor of everyday life. Can you find all 35 titles in the diagram?

A FAMILY TREE

AFTER THE PROM

ARTIST (The)

AT TEA TIME

BOOKWORM

CHAMP (The)

CHECKUP

CHRISTMAS EVE

CONNOISSEUR (The)

CRITIC (The)

DAYDREAMS

DINING OUT

DUGOUT (The)

FIXING A FLAT

GOING OUT

GOLDEN RULE (The)

GOSSIPS (The)

GRANDPA'S PRESENT

HOLDOUT (The)

HOME DUTY

HOME FROM VACATION

INTERVIEW (The)

LETTERMAN (The)

NATION'S HERO (The)

ON LEAVE

OUTING (The)

OUT OF A SCRAPE

PIANO TUNER

PLUMBERS (The)

PRIVATE CONCERT

PROM DRESS

SCHOLAR

SOLITAIRE

THANKSGIVING

TICKET AGENT

```
T R E V E S A M T S I R H C H E P C H I
E H L I L K N T I C O D I N I N G O U T
G E U M A P U G X H A L C W O R L N I A
S M R T U O G N I O G E I I X D E N S G
E R N T G R I S W L D G T T O S T O E R
K O E U Y A M E P A S A R U A Y T I N A
C W D B Y L I F R R C L T I C I E S R N
I K L T M V I P I A N O T U N E R S H D
T O O N R U S M V X S C P V T W M E O P
N O G E H K L M A R I M R T E O A U M A
A B T G B O O P T F A N E I R Y N R E S
T N Y A D R P Y E H A L G P T W X H D P
I K U T F L I R C A T T E A T I M E U R
O N L E A V E X O I S H U G F X C K T E
N U M K O N C E N M T R N E M L C E Y S
S O T C A O N O C R D A Y D R E A M S E
H T S I T R A K E G N R W O H I N T J N
E M P T N I S T R I Y D E C K X M L S T
R R Z V E G F O T H A N K S G I V I N G
O U T O F A S C R A P E G O S S I P S I
```

RECEIPT: MONTEREY ZUCCHINI

If you're planning a luncheon or light supper, try this recipe for Monterey Zucchini. Serve it with a salad and whole grain bread. Enjoy!

APPROXIMATELY	GRATE	SEASONINGS
BAKE	MELT	SERVINGS
BEAT	MINUTES	SET ASIDE
BOWL	ONION	SKILLET
BUTTER	OPTIONAL	STEAM
CASSEROLE DISH	OVER THE TOP	STIR
CHEESE	PEEL	TABLESPOONS
CHOPPED	PEPPER	TO TASTE
DICE	PINCH	UNTIL TENDER
EGG MIXTURE	PLACE	WARM
EGGS	POUR	WELL BLENDED
GARLIC SALT		

Monterey Zucchini

2 tablespoons butter
¼ cup onion, chopped
1 lb. zucchini
4 large eggs

pinch of onion salt
  (optional)
pinch of garlic salt
pepper, to taste
2 cups Monterey Jack cheese

Grate the cheese. Set aside. Melt the butter in a small skillet, add the onions, and fry. While the onions are frying, peel and dice the zucchini; then steam for approximately 5 minutes or until tender. In a medium-sized bowl, beat the eggs. Add the seasonings and cheese. Stir just until well blended. Place zucchini and onions in a casserole dish, pour the egg mixture over the top, and bake at 350°F for approximately 20 minutes, or until the egg mixture is set. Serve warm. Makes 4-6 servings.

```
Y L E T A M I X O R P P A C L
D E D N E L B L L E W Q J A A
E T A B L E S P O O N S R S N
P A Q S B P I N C H K U G S O
P R J C E O O S T I R N E E I
O G B P H T T U L V I T G R T
H Q P E X E A L R N U I G O P
C E C J A H E S O N B L M L O
R I M M P T Q S I A A T I E N
D W R L L R A M E D K E X D I
R L A Q R E T T U B E N T I O
V C W J S V G L B Z P D U S N
E T S A T O T G E O Q E R H L
I S G N I V R E S M W R E Q J
J Q R G A R L I C S A L T L G
```

Although English writers like Sir Arthur Conan Doyle and Agatha Christie seem to dominate mystery fiction, the contributions of American writers cannot be overlooked. From Dashiell HAMMETT and Ellery QUEEN to today's Sara PARETSKY and Tony HILLERMAN, American mysteries have attracted a large and devoted following. Track down the mystery writers hidden below; you'll have fun ''solving'' this one!

ALLEN (Steve)
BARNES (Linda)
BRAUN (Lillian Jackson)
BURNS (Rex)

CARR (John Dickson)
CHANDLER (Raymond)
CLARK (Mary Higgins)
CORNWELL (Patricia D.)

CRANE (Frances)
DAVIS (Dorothy Salisbury)
DUNLAP (Susan)
FORD (Leslie)
FULTON (Eileen)
GARDNER (Erle Stanley)
GRAFTON (Sue)
HALL (Parnell)
HAMMETT (Dashiell)
HESS (Joan)
HILLERMAN (Tony)
KAYE (Marvin)
LATHEN (Emma)
LUTZ (John)
MACDONALD (John D.)
MCBAIN (Ed)
PAGE (Katherine Hall)
PARETSKY (Sara)
PARKER (Robert B.)
QUEEN (Ellery)
RICH (Virginia)
RINEHART (Mary Roberts)
SHANNON (Dell)
SPILLANE (Mickey)
STOUT (Rex)
TRUMAN (Margaret)
TYRE (Nedra)
UHNAK (Dorothy)

```
K D L A N O D C A M R W E M
H A B L T R A H E N I R N G
G Q N U L R V J T R U M A N
Y R O H F N I A B C M R L C
K T A K U Q S L R U D T L H
S B A F L A T H E N R L I I
T Y A Z T U L T E J O N P L
E N D R O O N R E L F Q S L
R T U X N O N N S M U L T E
A A N A N E A Q S E M Y G R
P L L N R R S R E K R A P M
K R A L C B Z N H E P I H A
W H P R E L D N A H C J C N
S L C O R N W E L L A H Y H
```

Monty Python fans may remember the sketch in which a chorus sang the praises of Spam. In Texas there's a whole festival devoted to the canned meat. Or maybe that's just an excuse for having a party.

Among the major cultural events of the year is the annual Spam Festival in Austin, Texas, each spring. Activities include a Spam-tossing competition and the Spam-calling contest, won last year with the cry, ''Spammy, Spammy, Spammy, Spammy!''

```
A T H E C R Y E A R W H O Y
Z Y H C I A M A P S O G Y R
V U M J A N M T Z F N O O Q
C C M M I E A Z O O L J U S
U J O X A L P U M S A X E T
L Y M M A P S A S M S I V E
T C X U P Z S S E T T I E J
U O N R A E Y H P I I B N G
R N X F E S T I V A L N T G
A T O H S D R I X O M H S N
L E T F N P T C T Q T M X I
H S J A T C A L L I N G Y R
I T W U A H V M W Q O R P P
A B L I O U E D U L C N I S
```

In the United States there is approximately one telephone number for every two people. Here's an amusing story about an occasion when phone service was disrupted.

When a
major
phone
outage
left
much
of New
York
City
without
service,
the phone
company
explained
later
that the
power
to a
switching
office
went out,
and the
staff
in that
office
were
all off
that
day—at a
class on
what
to do
if the
power
failed!

```
E C I V R E S K C S T A F F
S C P O W E R X Y W F D U Q
W H I Z O O X E E E E Y U T
I B L F Y U O N W N L N O Z
T H A T F Z T F I O X A J A
C L A S S O N A C H P P B T
H W G Q U I L I G P U M U A
I H C T Z P T L X E X O X Y
N E X Y X Y J E A H H C S A
G N H E U Q C D V T S C N D
T A H T N I V U I T E D U M
A B L U F O W W H A T R Y M
W E N F O I H C S H O I E X
K R O J A M B P E T O D O W
```

Each term below has a number following it in parentheses, which refers to the numbered dashes below the diagram. Each word forms a box, reading clockwise or counterclockwise. (FRICTION has already been boxed to start you off.) As you find each term in the diagram, enter the unused letter that's in the middle of each box on the correspondingly numbered dash below the diagram ("E" has already been entered). When you have finished, the letters on the dashes will spell out the first two fillies to have won the Kentucky Derby.

ACTIVITY (8)

BAKESHOP (3)

CALENDAR (19)

CASHMERE (14)

DECOROUS (5)

DELEGATE (20)

DETECTOR (10)

EMPHASIS (6)

FRACTION (17)

~~FRICTION~~ (2)

HOMEWORK (9)

ICEBERGS (7)

MEGALITH (15)

MONOPOLY (4)

ORDINARY (13)

PEDIGREE (1)

REPORTER (16)

SELECTED (12)

VISUALLY (11)

YOURSELF (18)

```
I L W O R E S I R F E S D
T A E D K R U O A I L A C
H P M O H S I Y C L E S R
A T E P G E L F V E N D A
S I S B A K E D E C T E S
L A U A T E D S E O H O U
L E S K E G R U O R O Y E
Y V I T C T O P E D U R G
Y M O E I V R E R I N A I
L R N F R K T E R G P E D
O P O R A Y T B A S H T I
G S I T C N I E C I M N L
E M O H T I V S E R E G A
```

E																			
1	2	3	4	5	6		7	8	9		10	11	12	13	14	15	16		17	18	19	20

DISTANT DANCES ———————— 140

These dances date back as far as 1512 (the MORRIS dance). Many of them are still danced today, including the HORA, HULA and POLKA. Get into the groove and find 32 dances from the past.

ALLEMANDE (1685) COURANTE (1586) GALOP (1831)

BOLERO (1787) CZARDAS (1860) GAVOTTE (1696)

BOURRÉE (1706) FANDANGO (1774) HABANERA (1878)

CLOG (1869) FLAMENCO (1896) HORA (1878)

COTILLION (1776) GALLIARD (1533) HULA (1825)

JIG (1560)

JUBA (1834)

LANCER (1590)

MAZURKA (1818)

MINUET (1673)

MORRIS (dance, 1512)

PAVANE (1535)

POLKA (1844)

POLONAISE (1800s)

REEL (1585)

RIGADOON (1691)

RUMBA (1922)

SAMBA (1885)

SARABAND (1616)

SQUARE (dance, 1878)

TANGO (1913)

WALTZ (1712)

```
S G A L L I A R D B P L R E
D Q P B C Z T W H O R A T D
O M U O M J U B A L F N E N
S A R A B A N D M E A C V A
E Z I K R D S O G R P E S M
S N G L E E R R U O B R A E
I Z A P O R N O L W L Z D L
A T D V I V C A M Q U C R L
N L O S A N G N B R S M A A
O A O G E P O L K A O I Z R
L W N M N F L A J U H N C U
O F A N D A N G O I Q U S M
P L H B E T T O V A G E L B
F A N O I L L I T O C T K A
```

162

Fans of Jackie Gleason's variety show may remember the opening production numbers performed by the June TAYLOR Dancers. Step lively through this puzzle and find TAYLOR and 37 other choreographers.

AILEY (Alvin)
ASHTON (Frederick)
BENNETT (Michael)
BETTIS (Valerie)
CARLISLE (Kevin)
CHAMPION (Gower)
COLE (Jack)
CRANKO (John)
DALE (Grover)
DEAN (Laura)
DOLLY (Jenny)
FAISON (George)
FALCO (Louis)
FLATT (Ernest)
FOSSE (Bob)
FRANCA (Celia)
FRANKEL (Emily)
GENNARO (Peter)
GEVA (Tamara)
GRAHAM (Martha)
GRECO (José)
HANEY (Carol)
HUMPHREY (Doris)
JOFFREY (Robert)
LABAN (Rudolf von)
LAYTON (Joe)

LIFAR (Serge)
LIMÓN (José)
LORING (Eugene)
MOISEYEV (Igor)
MONK (Meredith)
PETIPA (Marius)

PETIT (Roland)
ROBBINS (Jerome)
TAYLOR (June)
THARP (Twyla)
TUNE (Tommy)
VILLELLA (Edward)

```
G Y L Y E R H P M U H T S V
R E W F B Q U A G A U Y N I
C N V H R L H E K N O M I L
T A L A B A N P E T I T B L
T H F O R A N N E G N R B E
A I A G J P O K N A R C O L
L C A R L I S L E J O E R L
F M C D P T I D O L L Y C A
H D N M A E A F E A Y Z S O
I L A E I P F O N Y A H D C
U H R L L R O S I T T E B L
C W F V E Y E S I O M K I A
E S T Y Y T T E N N E B N F
```

Duke Paoa Kahinu Makoe Hulikohola Kahanamoku (1890–1968) is known as the "Father of Surfing." He was a Hawaiian Olympic gold medalist swimmer who popularized surfing in California during a 1911 visit. Since then, surfing culture has developed a wild and wacky vocabulary of hundreds of words and phrases. We've hidden some of them below.

AGGRO
ARCH
AUSSIE

AXED
BAIL
BANZAI

BARNEY
BARREL
BIFF
BOGUS
CHOKE
COMBER
DISMO
FOIL
GNARLY
GROMMET
HANG TEN
JUNKER
KAHUNA
KOOK
LATRONIC
LOOMER
MONDO
NECTAR
PEAK
PIPELINE
REEDS
RHINO
SCUNGIES
STOKED
TUBED
ZONKED

```
C O M B E R J S L K O L Z P
M L B D H A A P T F O M O E
A B A I L N S U G O B O N K
R J N T U C V G M I K I K D
C O Z H R H R E N L L E E L
P E A K A O R S W E X O D S
D K I O M K N E P H C R A D
N A M M G E B I F F P T L E
E D E F A D P G C M Q J A E
A T E N E T G N A H O U P R
B G I X U N S U K E S N O T
O J G B A H U C S S M K D E
S L E R G O M S I D A E R O
W D L P O T F E B A R R E L
V Y E N R A B L S O P M I Q
```

ANSWERS

1 2 3

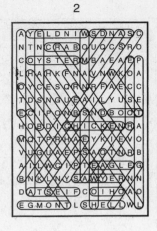
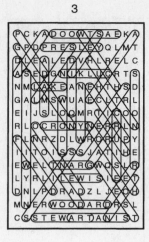

4 5 6

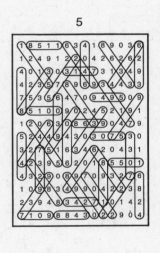
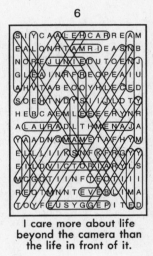
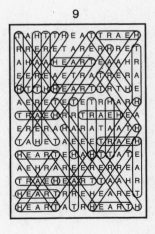

Moses Coats

I care more about life
beyond the camera than
the life in front of it.

7 8 9

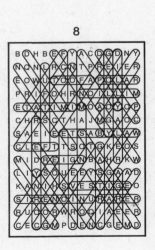

10

11

12

15

13

14

18

16

17

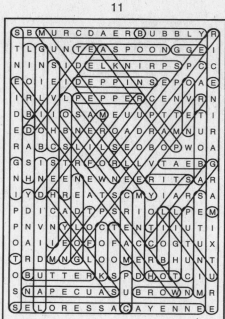

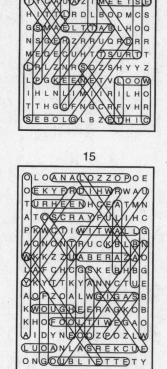

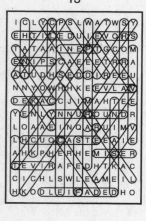

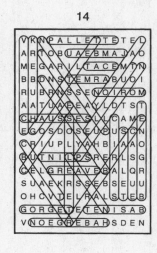

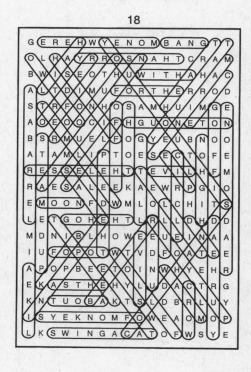

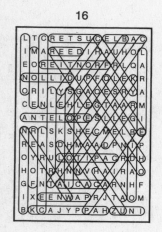

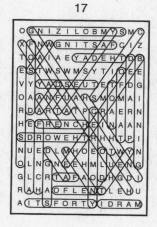

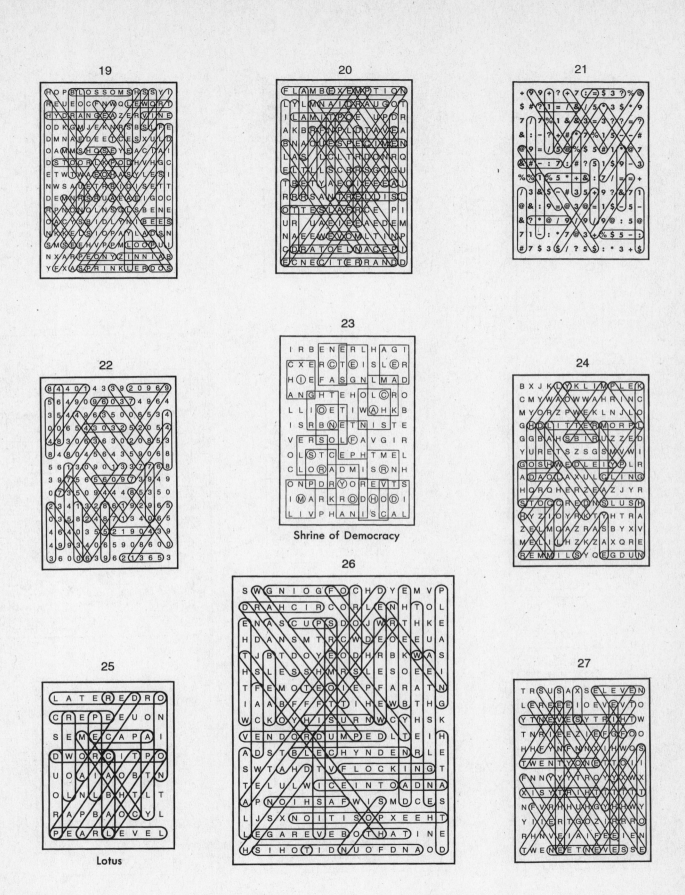

19

20

21

23

Shrine of Democracy

22

24

25

Lotus

26

27

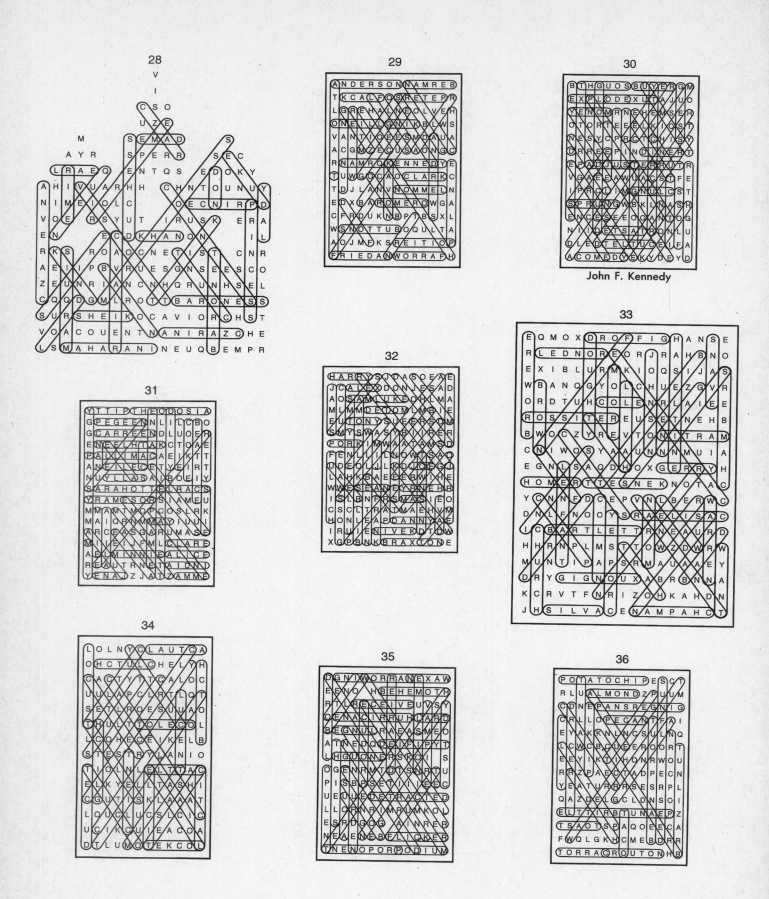

30 — John F. Kennedy

170

37

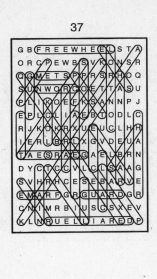

38

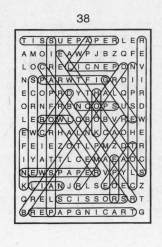

39

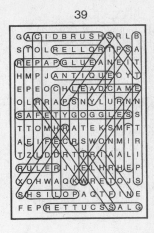

40

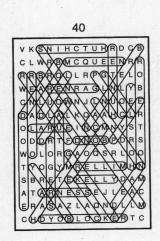

41

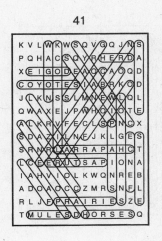

42

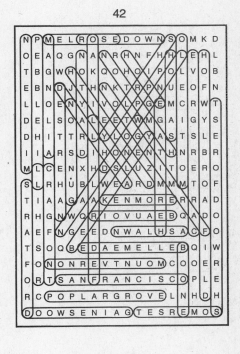

43

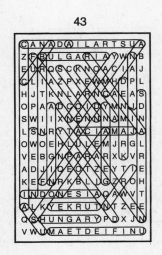

44

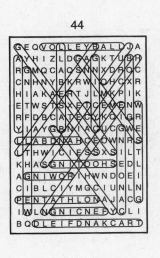

45

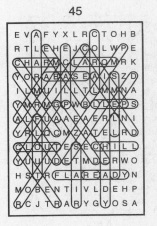

46

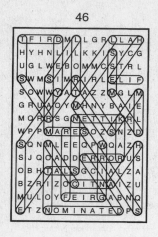

47

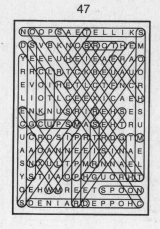

48

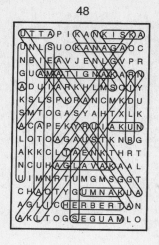

49

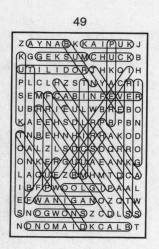

50

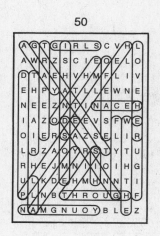

51

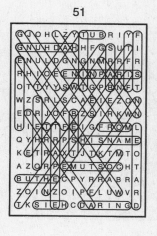

52

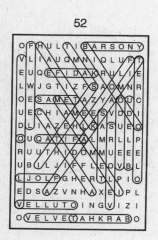

53

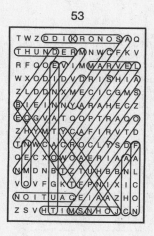

54

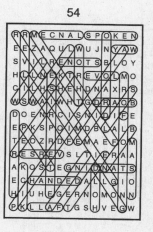

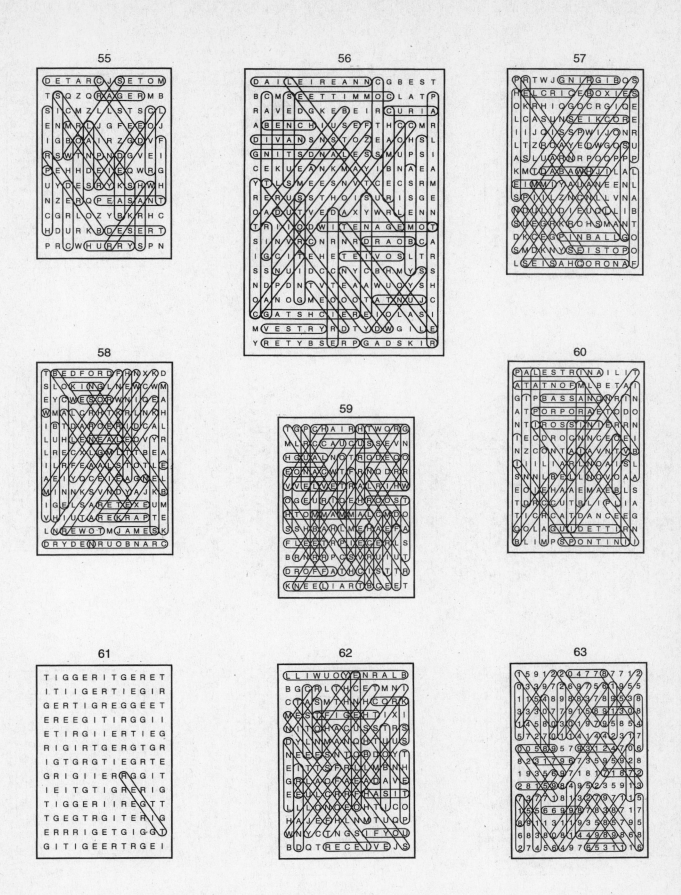

64

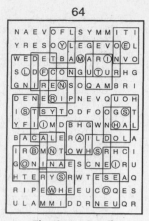

*The Swiss Family
Robinson*

65

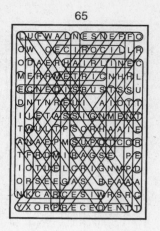

66

67

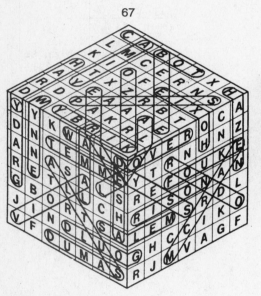

68

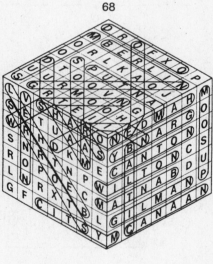

69

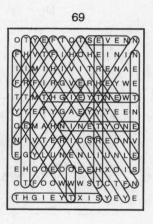

70

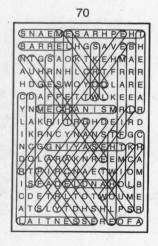

71

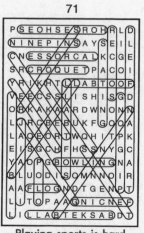

**Playing sports is hard
work for which you do
not get paid.**

72

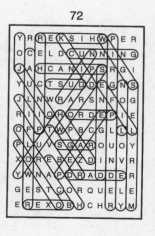

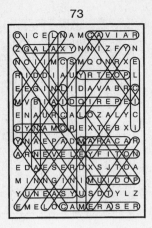

73

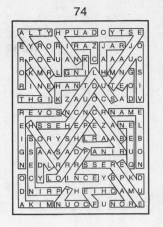

74

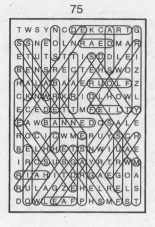

75

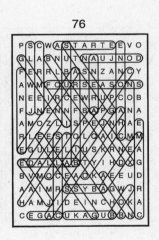

76

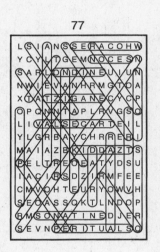

77

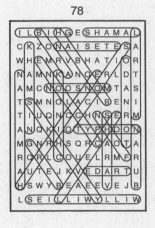

78

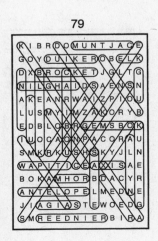

79

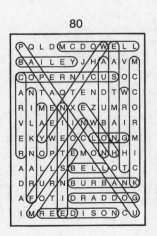

80

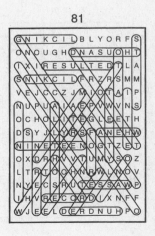

81

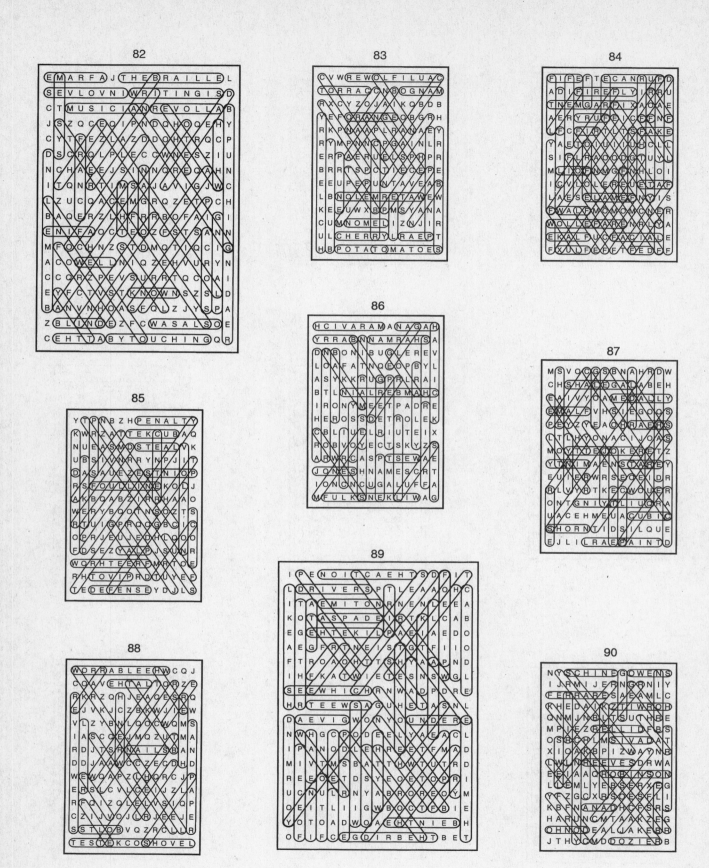

82

83

84

85

86

87

88

89

90

176

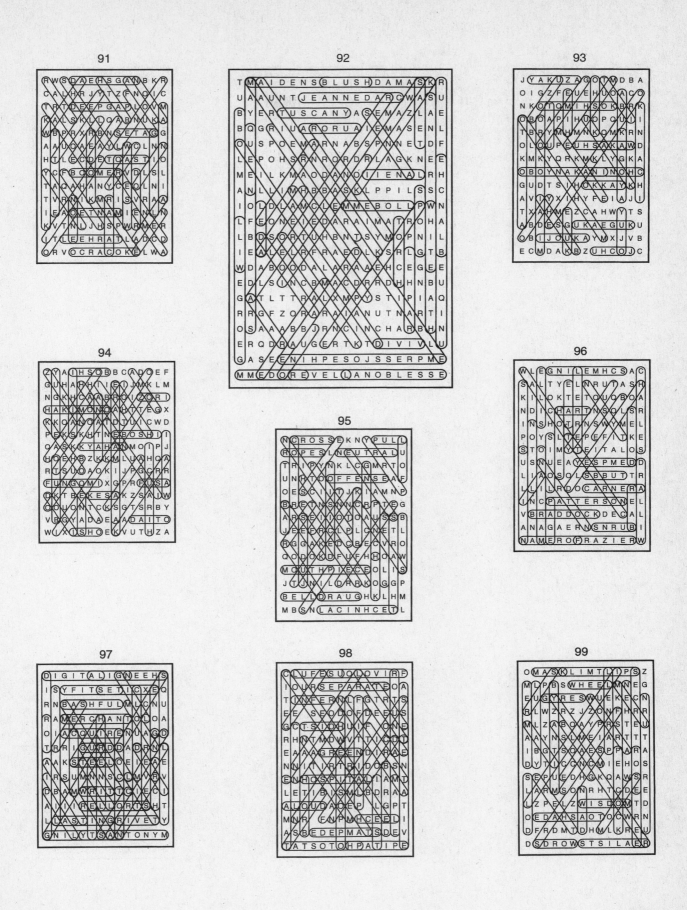

100

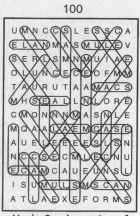

Uncle Sam's version of
"Truth or Consequences"
is a tax form.

101

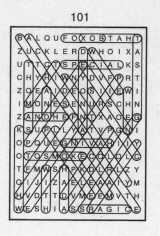

102

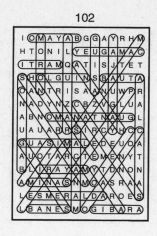

103

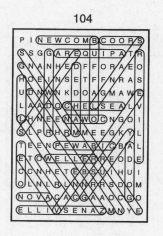

104

105

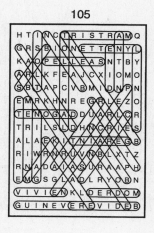

106

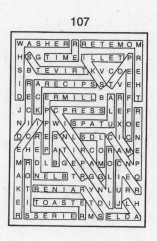

107

108

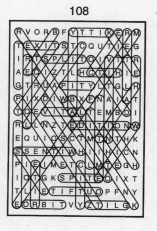

109

The happiness of society is the end of government.

110

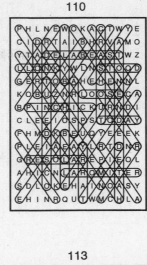

111

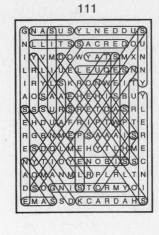

112

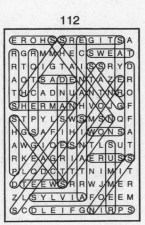

113

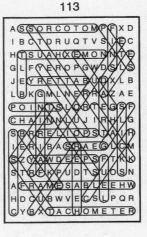

114

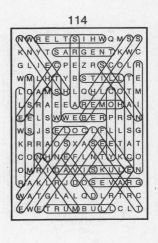

115

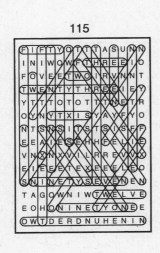

116

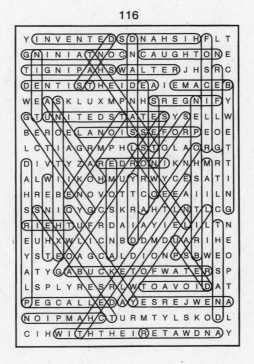

117

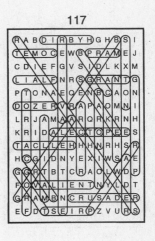

118

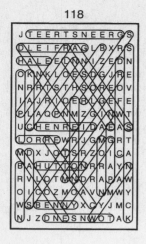

119

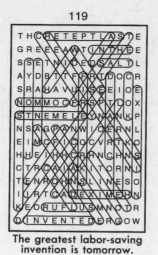

The greatest labor-saving invention is tomorrow.

120

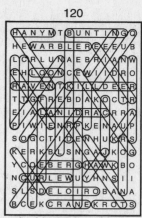

The bluebird carries the sky on his back.

121

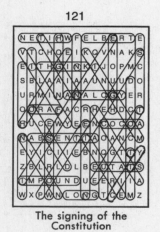

The signing of the Constitution

122

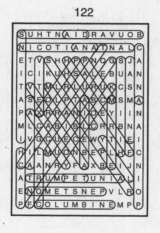

123

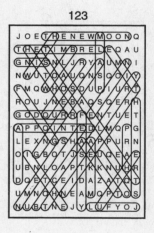

124

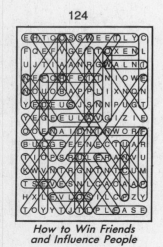

How to Win Friends and Influence People

125

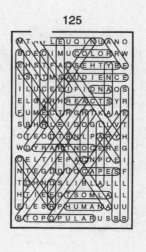

126

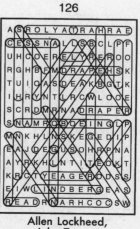

Allen Lockheed, John Towers

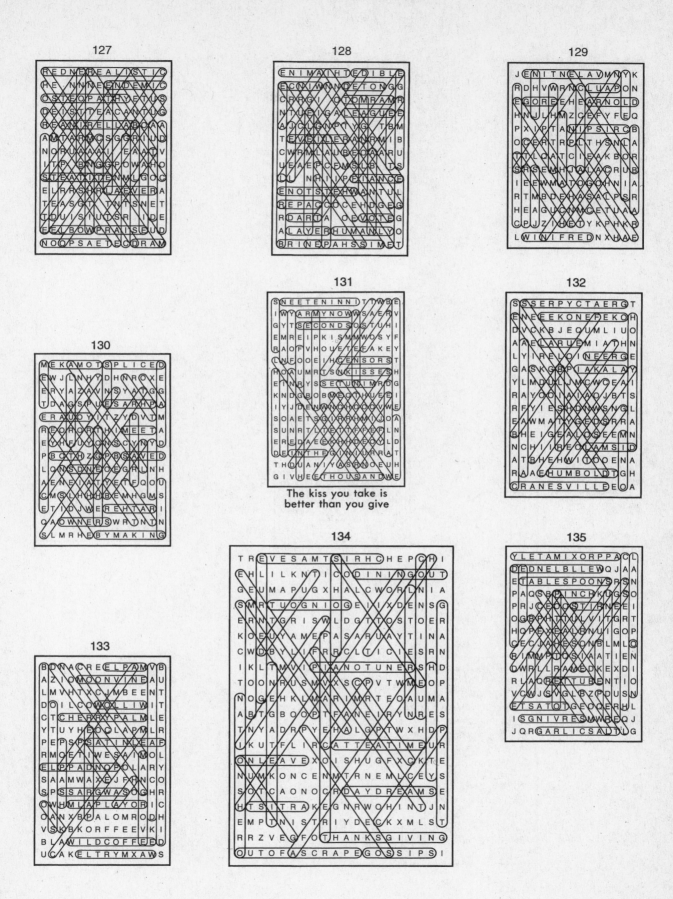

The kiss you take is
better than you give

136

137

138

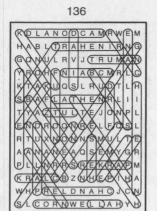
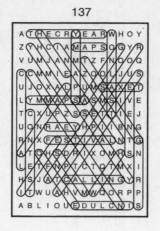
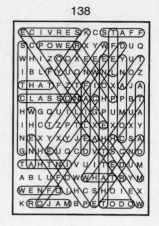

139

140

141

Regret and Genuine Risk

142

3 THEY FILMED IN FLORIDA 1. Creature From the Black Lagoon 2. Paper Lion 3. Cocoon 4. Cocoon 5. Days of Thunder 6. My Girl 7. Licence to Kill 8. Caddyshack 9. Cape Fear 10. Edward Scissorhands 11. Revenge of the Creature 12. Absence of Malice 13. Honky Tonk Freeway 14. Don't Drink the Water 15. Operation Petticoat 16. The Greatest Show on Earth 17. Body Heat 18. The Greatest Show on Earth 19. Wind Across the Everglades 20. Slattery's Hurricane 21. The Bellboy 22. Clambake 23. Edward Scissorhands 24. Jaws 3-D 25. Smokey and the Bandit II 26. Semi-Tough 27. Stick 28. Tony Rome 29. Passenger 57 30. Strategic Air Command 31. Doc Hollywood 32. Cross Creek 33. Lady in Cement 34. Parenthood 35. On an Island With You 36. Cross Creek 37. Night Moves 38. The Yearling 39. Neptune's Daughter

6 SO YOU WANT TO BE IN PICTURES 1. Agnes 2. Alice 3. Annie 4. Bernadette 5. Beverly 6. Clementine 7. Daisy 8. Dolly 9. Eileen 10. Emily 11. Eve 12. Georgy 13. Gidget 14. Hannah 15. Irma 16. Jane 17. Jean 18. Judy 19. Junie 20. Katie 21. Kitty 22. Laura 23. Lily 24. Mame 25. Mary 26. Mildred 27. Molly 28. Peggy Sue 29. Rachel 30. Rita 31. Rose 32. Rosemary 33. Sally 34. Sara 35. Sheena 36. Sophie 37. Tiffany 38. Victoria

9 + AND x SEARCH 5 letters afoot + irony, again x meaty, aglow x polka, agree + rarer, alley x piled, apply x moped, baste + mason, bylaw + relay, cared x sired, cleft + reedy, color x molar, corny + siren, curio x moral, dilly + polar, drive + union, erase x shaft, fruit x mound, grove x shore, miner x rinse, reign + suite. **7 letters** cartoon x section, consent x erosion, economy x granite, fistful + imitate, gastric + vestige, geology + million, outgrow x stagger.

11 TAIL TAG Prime, esteem, mold, dusting, globes, still, legal, lumber, rack, kilt, trunk, keen, nice, ethic, crow, wool, lift, tries, stub, battle, etch, hula, aroma, after, raze, escort, trust, tonic, clench, help, press, stamped, dormer, roll, lint, tabs, solo, octet, time.

13 JACKPOT Ankle, antic, armed, asked, caked, caste, cease, chant, cheep, chick, choke, cinch, clash, couch, count, creed, daily, faded, field, inept, itchy, knack, laser, latch, lithe, mauve, miser, munch, plait, rated, raver, rivet, round, runny, saint, shelf, shirr, shore, shove, spine, super, tally, tepee, tiled, valve, venue, verge, verve, vista, wiped, yacht.

20 PHRASE PLAY As much fun as a barrel of monkeys, As the crow flies, Better safe than sorry, Cold hands warm heart, Come full circle, Finish with a bang, Get all steamed up about, Go off the deep end, Hail fellow well met, In apple pie order, Keep it under your hat, Live high on the hog, Not enough room to swing a cat, Off the top of your head, Put your money where your mouth is, Read someone like a book, Shoot for the moon, Tell it to the Marines, The lesser of two evils.

24 TAIL TAG Prom, music, cling, gridlock, kelp, pill, levy, yield, dues, slush, haven, nudge, easy, yaks, slimmer, relic, cool, lard, draw, worth, helm, mimic, cots, shag, gosh, heal, litter, rump, plank, keel, load, dough, howl, lower, ribs, steam, milky, yard, date.

27 MATH FUN 1. sixty-two 2. five 3. eleven 4. eight 5. seven 6. thirty-six 7. three 8. eighty-three 9. five 10. sixty 11. thirty-one 12. seventy-three 13. five 14. sixty-one 15. two 16. four 17. thirty-seven 18. eighty-nine 19. six 20. three 21. eighty 22. forty 23. five 24. seventy 25. seventeen 26. five 27. eighty-two 28. three 29. twenty-one

34 TLC Actual, blotch, cartel, castle, cattle, chalet, claret, client, closet, clothe, clutch, costly, curtly, cutely, cutler, cutlet, dulcet, elicit, glitch, lactic, locate, locket, locust, lucent, occult, ocelot, sculpt, select, tackle, talcum, tickle.

40 OLD COWHANDS 1. Gunsmoke 2. The Gene Autry Show 3. Bat Masterson 4. Bonanza 5. Wagon Train 6. Hopalong Cassidy 7. Laredo 8. The Guns of Will Sonnett 9. The Young Riders 10. The Legend of Jesse James 11. The Rifleman 12. Trackdown 13. The Marshall of Gunsight Pass 14. Alias Smith and Jones 15. Rawhide 16. The Dakotas 17. Laramie 18. Maverick 19. Bonanza 20. The Virginian 21. Paradise 22. Temple Houston 23. Sugarfoot 24. Maverick 25. Bonanza 26. Lash of the West 27. The Big Valley 28. The Adventures of Wild Bill Hickok 29. Wanted: Dead or Alive 30. The Young Riders 31. The Lone Ranger 32. The Life and Legend of Wyatt Earp 33. The Cisco Kid 34. Tales of Wells Fargo 35. The Roy Rogers Show 36. The Dakotas

45 + AND x SEARCH Abase + place, alarm + charm, amend x trend, blame x claim, blimp x crimp, burly x curly, chill + drill, clout + flout, comma x mamma, coral + moral, cuter x tutor, dully x gully, flare + stair, gazed x lazed, heady + ready, lease x peace, smell + spell.

46 TAIL TAG File, etch, hall, limit, troll, lies, swarm, mares, sprains, squash, hula, antic, clam, motion, nominated, dance, error, rank, kitten, needs, slat, true, emboss, spray, yield, drift, thus, sour, roar, rants, skim, meld, dram, mess, scram, meow, wring, grief, folder.

55 LOOSE LETTERS Sallow, cased, lines, lands, baked, lodge, other, border, money, motes, cured, peasant, hurry, fight, pries, ridge, waker, punch, rager, hares, desert, sings, scrap, crated, cover. **PROVERB:** Hunger makes hard beans sweet.

69 MATH FUN 1. fifty-nine 2. eighty 3. five 4. ninety 5. twenty-eight 6. four 7. sixty-eight 8. ninety 9. five 10. sixty 11. two 12. ninety-one 13. thirty-three 14. ninety-nine 15. thirty-eight 16. three 17. twelve 18. fifty-one 19. seven 20. thirteen 21. four 22. eighty 23. five 24. fifty 25. seventeen 26. thirty-one 27. three

53 HOMOPHONE HALVES Adds, band, breech, choir, chute, dear, entrance, flour, grizzly, hair, leaf, mast, phrase, slow, steak, sun, surge, tract, waste.

88 PRODUCING PRODUCE 1. Apple 2. Banana 3. Bean 4. Beet 5. Blueberry 6. Cabbage 7. Carrot 8. Cauliflower 9. Cherry 10. Cocoanut 11. Corn 12. Cucumber 13. Grape 14. Huckleberry 15. Lemon 16. Lime 17. Mango 18. Onion 19. Orange 20. Peach 21. Pear 22. Peas 23. Pepper 24. Pineapple 25. Plum 26. Potato 27. Prune 28. Raisin 29. Strawberry 30. Tomatoes 31. Watermelon.

87 JACKPOT Alder, badge, carry, chimp, clash, clasp, cruet, cubic, dally, enjoy, equip, etude, flame, glove, hated, holed, jerky, jetty, joker, legal, loner, medal, minty, octet, onset, paint, pearl, quilt, quire, raced, radio, rajah, rouse, runty, satyr, shale, shame, shear, shirr, shoal, shorn, short, slyly, stare, strew, thyme, totem, tying, vinyl

88 SCRAMBLED HARDWARE 1. bolts 2. bucket 3. chisel 4. drill 5. file 6. hammer 7. hose 8. ladder 9. lathe 10. lawn mower 11. level 12. nails 13. pliers 14. rake 15. sandpaper 16. screwdriver 17. shovel 18. socket set 19. stapler 20. table saw 21. tool chest 22. vise 23. wheelbarrow 24. wire 25. workbench 26. wrench

89 PHRASE PLAY Be in the driver's seat; call a spade a spade; carry a torch for; easy come easy go; get a piece of the action; give a piece of your mind; have a sweet tooth; heading for a fall; like a fish out of water; no time like the present; play both ends against the middle; put your heads together; read between the lines; see which way the wind blows; take it in stride; the whole kit and caboodle; throw good money after bad; trip the light fantastic; water under the bridge.

103 TAIL TAG Slap, polo, orange, exit, trim, molar, rusted, drink, kittens, sham, mint, toll, lumps, swell, lead, drama, ankle, eraser, round, dill, longer, relaxing, gala, arts, seams, swig, grins, sleigh, hoop, poker, rule, ends, string, golden, never, rave, each, herons, stick.

108 GET WITH "IT" Ability, admit, alit, await, bite, blithe, citadel, cite, city, ditch, ditto, edition, emit, exit, flit, gait, glitz, habit, hitch, itch, item, itself, kite, kitty, knit, limit, liter, loiter, mite, mitten, omit, orbit, outfit, pity, polite, quite, respite, rite, site, spirit, spite, split, title, tuition, vital, vitamin, waiter, white, wither, witness.

110 + AND x SEARCH Adder x order, alert x obese, arise + chick, arson x essay, aside x prior, astir x motor, atone + stood, baled + bylaw, baron x early, bayou x layer, beast + crash, belle + solar, borne x curly, broad + knoll, disco + loser, ended + today, fleck x sheik, glare x piano, hated + miter, hider x pedal, homey x timid, lance x pinon, loose + shout, moral + tarry, pinch + tuned, plush x usual, seedy x trend.

184